CONTENTS

STAFFORDSHIRE LIBRARY AND INFORMATION SERVICES
Please return or renew by the last date shown

If not required by other readers, this item may be renewed in person, by post or telephone, online or by email.
To renew, either the book or ticket are required

24 HOUR RENEWAL LINE 0845 33 00 740

CROWOOD SPORTS GUIDES
MOUNTAIN BIKING
SKILLS · TECHNIQUES · TRAINING

James McKnight

THE CROWOOD PRESS

First published in 2012 by
The Crowood Press Ltd
Ramsbury, Marlborough
Wiltshire SN8 2HR

www.crowood.com

British Library Cataloguing-in-Publication Data
A catalogue record for this book is available from the British Library.

ISBN 978 1 84797 419 8

Acknowledgements
A special thanks to photographer Chris Jackson of Kingdom Bikes for his great photography.
Also thanks to Bertie Maffoon's bike shop in Marlborough, Wiltshire for help with the maintenance sections.
Thank you to my family, friends and to Isobel for helping me with my efforts.
And for their help, thank you to Trek, Osprey, Teva, Royal and The North Face.

Photography by Chris Jackson/kingdombike.

Typeset by Jean Cussons Typesetting, Diss, Norfolk
Printed and bound in Singapore by Craft Print International Ltd

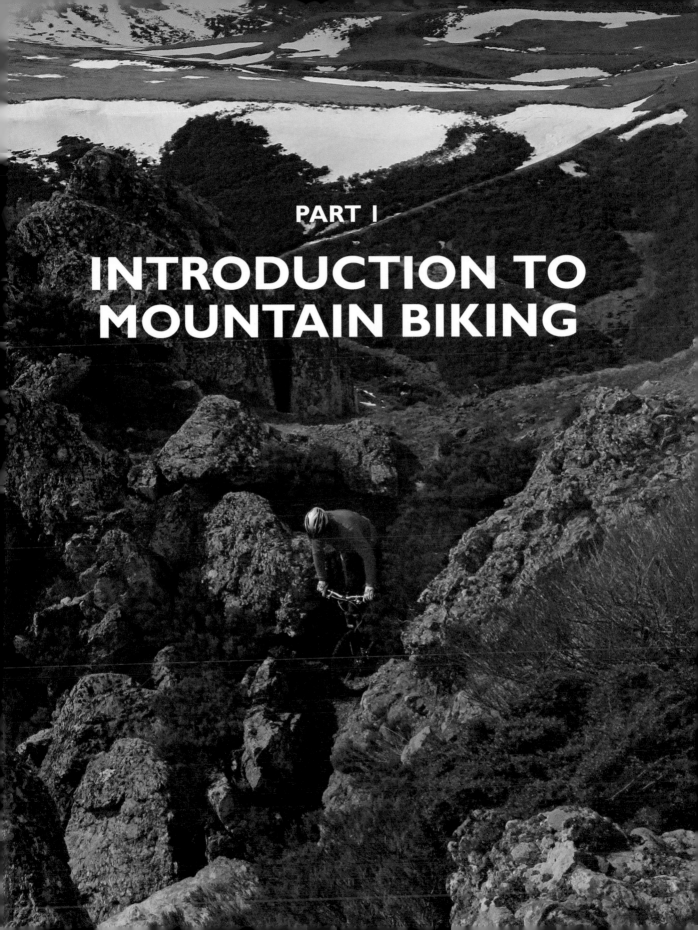

PART I
INTRODUCTION TO MOUNTAIN BIKING

CHAPTER I

HISTORY OF THE SPORT

Introduction to Mountain Biking

Mountain biking is the off-road form of cycling that has become widespread over the last two decades and is fast becoming the most popular two-wheeled sport. Accessible to all ages, fitness and skill levels, a year-round sport and applicable to any location – hillside or plateau – mountain biking is perhaps the most versatile sport of the moment.

History

Bicycles have been ridden off-road ever since their invention; however, the first recordings of 'mountain biking' are hazily recounted from somewhere in the late 1970s when a group of hippies in Marin County, USA, began to take their '*klunkerz*' (beach cruisers) to the hills and race down dirt tracks.

During the 1980s, the term 'mountain bike' was coined and Gary Fisher started to produce geared off-road bicycles. From what started so humbly, the sport soon became a craze and by the early 1990s there were televised events, professional riders and a global race series.

Mountain biking is for everyone; it's fun, healthy and environmentally friendly.

The sport's founders pushed and carried their basic bikes up mountains in the USA.

That craze died off somewhat around the middle of the decade. However, the sport continued to thrive and progress, with new technologies constantly developing the sport and feeding a hungry consumer market. Currently the sport is having a rebirth as adventurers and families alike begin to realize the potential of the modern mountain bike, with an increasing number of trail centres and summer resorts creating an ever-growing abundance of biking terrain, and paving the way for future generations of mountain bikers.

Early Competitions

Mountain biking was born as a competition sport and yet only considered mildly competitively natured. The majority of riders were hippies and the race meeting was considered more important than the racing itself. However, with the increase in popularity and the invention of the saleable mountain bike, the sport sprouted many high-profile competitions, some of which continue to run to this day:

- Fat Tyre Festivals were huge events that originated in the USA and that included all the fanfare of a music festival. The most famous event took place in Moab, Utah and paved the way for the place to become one of the most visited mountain bike destinations in the world.
- The UCI World Cup commenced in 1989 and has since included disciplines such as dual slalom, dual, four-cross, downhill, trials and cross-country; the latter three of which comprise the modern day series.
- The first World Championships took place in 1990 in Durango, Colorado with the winners taking home the now much-coveted rainbow striped jersey. The 'Worlds' is the most important single event on the mountain bike calendar and some racers focus their entire season on the one event.
- The Kamikaze Downhill is a now legendary race that took place on Mammoth Mountain, USA. The event was a head-to-head eliminator race down the high-speed fire-roads on the mountainside and claimed many casualties, eventually leading to its retirement from the racing calendar.
- National Championships now take place the world over, mostly on the same date so as not to clash with international racing commitments – the exception to this rule is for some southern-hemisphere countries who prefer to host their championships in the middle of their summers.
- The Malvern Classic was once the biggest event on the UK calendar and brought riders from all disciplines together at a site in the Malvern Hills. This event had a true festival atmosphere with various races taking place over the course of the event and on-site bars, live music and camping for all.
- The Olympics first accepted mountain biking to the roster in 1996 and the event has been a huge success. Only cross-country racing is included in the mountain bike Olympics but the majority of riders also hope to see downhill brought to the event.

Mountain biking is a world-wide sport.

- New Zealand has the terrain and the attitude to sport that is needed for mountain biking and, unsurprisingly, is one of the strongest nations in terms of racing results: Justin Leov and Cameron Cole are two of the most successful riders of the moment. Although more sparse than in the UK, there are 'bike parks' and trails appearing all over the country making it the top winter destination for all bike riders.
- Australia is a true sporting nation, which puts a lot of money into funding for its future sports stars. Mountain biking is no exception with many top athletes including Cadel Evans (who now races in road cycling), Sam Hill and Chris Kovarik. However, facilities are minimal in comparison to other leading countries and there is little in the way of prepared trails.
- The USA continues to push the sport forward in terms of technology, and many thousands of mountain bikers travel from the world over to ride in famous destinations such as Moab and Mammoth. Aaron Gwin is the downhill star who currently dominates

Names and Nations

Mountain biking was invented in the USA and the country has always had a strong presence on the mountain bike scene, but these days there are other nations who dominate the sport with higher participation figures and champions across the sport's disciplines.

- The UK has one of the highest participation rates in the world along with some of the best infrastructure, both of which create a huge amount of revenue from the sports tourism they create. There are dozens of 'trail-centres' (dedicated bike destinations with all-weather, purpose built trails) in the UK, which generate millions of pounds for the economy. The sport is fronted by hugely successful riders, particularly in downhill – the likes of which include Steve Peat, Gee Atherton and Danny Hart.

Technology is always advancing.

the sport, and is the true American dream kid.

- France and Switzerland contain some of the best bike riding in the world and subsequently attract tourists from the world over for the summer opening months, June to September, when the ski lift systems are open to bikes. France in particular has long been producing top riders, with the sport's most successful racers ever, Nicolas Vouilloz and Anne-Caroline Chausson, being most notable.
- Canada does not produce a great number of competitive cyclists, but what it lacks in champions it more than makes up for in its cutting-edge bike-parks. Whistler is the most popular destination in the world for mountain biking and attracts cyclists from all over the world during its long summer opening (open from May until late October).

Progression of Technology

Mountain bikes have been at the cutting-edge of bicycle design ever since their invention, and their constant development continues to forge new technologies to this day. Where once, in the early 1990s, it was considered state-of-the-art, even unnecessary by some, to have full-suspension on a mountain bike, today manufacturers are playing with space-age materials and experimenting with weight-saving, even aerodynamic, frame qualities. Modern suspension can be fine-tuned or locked-out at the flick of a switch, tyres are tubeless and nearly all bikes have hydraulic disc-brake systems.

Manufacturers are still experimenting though, with the latest trend being toward wheel sizes. Current theories state that bigger wheels will roll over rough ground more easily, and some manufacturers have almost entirely switched their range of bikes to bigger wheels. Whether this wheel size – 29in – will stay is an on-going debate in the sport and both conventional (26in) and large 'wagon-wheels' certainly do have their advantages and disadvantages.

The Alps hold some of the best mountain bike terrain in the world.

CHAPTER 2

STARTING OUT

Introduction

Starting out in any new sport can be daunting, and with the range of equipment available, the places to ride and the techniques in mountain biking being numerous, it could seem like one of the hardest sports to learn. However, people who ride bikes are friendly and bike shops will always take the time to explain, so the first rule to remember is to never fear to ask questions.

There are many subcategories within mountain biking, all of which are specialized factions of the sport's original concept, which was to be able to pedal up and ride down any trail, anywhere. General mountain biking – riding around cross-country circuits – is participant friendly and attracts the majority of the sport's riders. However, downhill riding and racing are most popular with the younger, adrenaline-

Mountain biking takes on many different guises.

seeking crowd and are also regarded at the forefront of the sport – the Formula One of cycling.

Types of Mountain Biking

Mountain Biking can be subdivided into many different categories, namely cross-country, downhill, trials and all-mountain riding. These divisions within the sport have become very specialist with most riders focusing their efforts on only one of the disciplines.

Cross-Country. This is how most people envisage mountain biking – riding on a range of terrain from tarmac to rock-fest, on lightweight and versatile bikes with a wide range of gears to take the rider up hill and down dale.

It is important to know the components of your bike.

Downhill. The gravity-fed, adrenaline-fuelled side of mountain biking comprises a younger crowd yet appeals visually to all. Tracks include daring leaps, daunting drops and high speeds.

Trials. Bicycle trials came about when the Spanish motor-cycle trials team were looking for another way to train and improve their skills. A small following soon developed, exploded in popularity and then crossed over into mountain biking, with riders such as Danny MacAskill now becoming household names.

All-Mountain. More recently coined, the term 'all-mountain' is used with reference to riding in more severe mountains, such as the Alps, where stronger bikes with front and rear suspension are needed to cope with the unforgiving terrain.

Cross-country bike. A 'hard-tail' has no rear suspension.

The Bikes

As much as the sport itself is diverse and varied, so too are the bikes. For each discipline there is a differing style of bike, and within each discipline's style of machine, each manufacturer has their own take on the design.

Understanding each and every brand within the sport is not necessary; however, it is important to understand the difference between each style of bike and to be able to gauge its designated purpose or discipline.

All-mountain/trail bike.

Trail/All-Mountain Bike

Trail bikes, also referred to as 'all-mountain' or 'enduro' bikes, are the most practical and all-encompassing mountain bikes on the market. These are designed to be able to cope with all conditions and to climb efficiently, whilst descending with the best – only a downhill-specific bike will descend better. Trail bikes are made for those who like to be out in the mountains riding technical trails or racing in endurance downhill competitions, but they are also suitable for UK Trail Centre riding and the bike of choice for most British riders.

Key features: single-crown forks; 2×10 gearing; 140–170mm suspension travel; height-adjust seatpost; robust tyres (2.35in width is generally preferred). *Purpose:* all-day riding. General mountain biking. Enduro downhill racing. *Price range:* £800+.

Downhill bike.

Single-speed bike.

Cross-Country Bike

Cross-country bikes are the machines that push the boundaries of weight, rolling resistance and materials. Designed with the fanatic in mind, these bikes are low-slung, a hard ride and have a large range of gearing; all aimed at making a bike that can climb fast, make it down the descents and that can be peddled at speed over long distances. Not the most comfortable or robust, but built with a purpose – speed. These bikes are more suited to those with a serious intention of racing and due to their lightweight nature, will stand up to far less abuse than trail or downhill orientated bikes.

Key features: lightweight (often carbon) frame; large range of gears (up to thirty); hard-tail or short-travel full suspension; low-profile, fast rolling tyres.
Purpose: pedalling efficiency; climbing speed; cross-country racing.
Price range: £500–£5,000.

Downhill Bike

As the name suggests, downhill bikes are made for going in one direction only – down. Laid-back chopper-like angles put the rider in a comfortable and confidence-inspiring position from which to attack even the steepest of slopes. Modern downhill bikes can cope with 10m jumps, speeds of over 50mph (80km/h) and severely rugged terrain. Not for going uphill, these are best suited to those living in mountainous areas with chairlift access or as a second bike for occasional uplift-aided riding.

Key features: relaxed angles; wide tyres; triple-clamp forks; low-slung top-tube; 200mm suspension travel.
Purpose: downhill riding and racing only.
Price range: £2,000+.

Single Speed

Single-speed bikes have only one gear, which eliminates a lot of products such as cables, derailleurs, gear shifters, etc., and in doing so creates a simplistic bike that can stand up to all conditions. These are generally hard-tail frames, as those wishing to ride with only one gear are normally looking for absolute simplicity.

Key features: one gear; hard-tail frame.
Purpose: low maintenance; fun.
Price range: £300+.

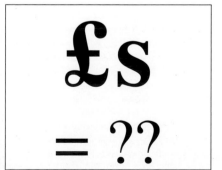

It is important to know where your money is going.

Guide to Buying a Bike

The mountain bike market is highly competitive amongst the numerous brands, which can range from innovative to imitators. The main brands within the industry can all be trusted to be providing quality manufacturing and components at a fair price. However, choosing a bike can still be a relative mine-field, so make sure that you understand the purposes of differing styles of bike (explained in Chapter 3) and take your time to invest in a steed that will last.

Follow the steps below to ensure a worth-while purchase.

Step 1: Decide Your Budget

We all have different budgets, but it is sensible to decide a high marker before you go shopping for a bike, and look for something close to your top price. More money does equal more bike.

- For under £500 you can get a quality front-suspension bike with disc brakes, sturdy wheels and a large range of gears.
- For £500–£1000 you will start to find lightweight, full suspension bikes with hydraulic disc brakes, twenty-seven gears and strong wheels.
- £1000–£1500 will buy you a quality bike with well-damped suspension, strong and lightweight wheels, up to thirty gears, hydraulic brakes and top-level ride quality.
- For £1500+ pretty much any bike purchased should have all of the above, plus discipline-specific features, such as lightweight carbon frames for cross-country riding, highly tuneable suspension for downhill and height-adjust seat-posts for all-mountain riding.

Step 2: Think Long-Term

Decide how keen you are to pursue the sport and therefore how serious you need your bike to be. Invest once in a bike that your abilities will not exceed within the first two years of riding. Full suspension will help you down more difficult trails but a hard-tail bike will improve your skills and offer much better components for your money.

Step 3: Features Checklist

Some bikes seem far below the price of something similar from competitors; this is not normally without reason. Check for the following to ensure you are buying the quality that you need:

- Tyres: if the rubber feels hard and plastic-like, then you will need to upgrade straight away, as the manufacturer has cut their costs by supplying a cheap imitation of the real thing. Good off-road tyres need to have strong side-walls and quality rubber in order to limit punctures and maximise grip.
- Brakes: hydraulic disc brakes are commonplace in mountain biking nowadays, so don't settle for anything less. If you have a low budget and opt for something without disc brakes, make sure that the bike has the available mounts for when you can afford to upgrade.
- Cheap components: particularly at the lower end of the price range, check that bikes don't have a large number of heavy steel components (check with a magnet) as these are cumbersome and will only need to be upgraded at a later date.

Step 4: Buy in Store

Although the internet can offer lower prices, the fitting service, advice and after-sales service of a bike shop cannot be beaten. Even if you do buy from an online store, you will most likely end up taking your bike to a shop to be checked over and serviced anyway and you will be charged where you would most likely not be, had you bought the bike from the shop.

Get to know your bike and you will soon be on your way to flowing trail riding.

Which Bike is Best?

It is impossible to label a bike the 'best', but bikes built by any of the major manufacturers at around the £1,000 price mark and with 120–140mm of suspension travel are ideal for everyday use and will stand up to serious riding.

TOP BRAND CHECKLIST

- GT: high technology, high prices.
- Santa Cruz: superb construction, top-quality finishing.
- Orange: English made, great construction and top-notch customer service.
- Trek: best range of bikes, great customer service and warranty department.
- Kona: cheaper but very functional bikes.
- Commencal: unbeatable attention to detail, great race bikes but not best for reliability.
- Intense: the Ferrari of mountain biking – no expenses spared, beautifully constructed machines.
- Specialized: one of the biggest brands and producers of an all-encompassing range of quality bikes.

Understanding Your Bike

It is important to understand your bike and to learn the names of the separate components, as this will make life a lot easier in the long run; you will be able to discuss points about set-up of your bike and altering the ride characteristics a lot more easily when you are speaking the same language as the rest of the bike world. It is also important to understand the uses and variables of each component.

Stem

The 'stem' is the component that attaches the handlebars to the top of the forks; the connecting piece of metal that takes care of steering duties. Stem length is variable between 30 and 90mm, with different lengths applicable to the differing disciplines, as well as the rider's height and dimensions.

Short stems are better for all-mountain and downhill riding, as they offer more direct steering and lessen flex. The majority of riders don't use anything more than a 50mm stem. For cross-country riding and racing, some prefer to use stems between 50 and 90mm in order to bring the rider into a 'flatter' and more stretched riding position, which is efficient for power output but uncomfortable over prolonged periods.

Handlebars

Steering is one area of your bike that you need to get right; the handlebars are your main control point for the bike. Another major factor to be considered is comfort, as the handlebars on your bike can affect your overall body position. Mountain bikers are tending to use wider and wider handlebars – the wider the bar, the more stable you should be – with the range now starting at 680mm and stretching to 780mm width (this is measured from end-to-end). However, everything relates back to body shape and intended purpose; the widest bars are only useful for the high speeds and wide courses that are found in downhill racing, and equally the narrowest are best left to serious cross-country racers who feel more comfortable climbing with narrow bars. For general/all-mountain riding, 720mm is now beginning to become a rough standard.

Shifters

The gear shifters are normally paddle-like components that 'hang' underneath the handlebars. The shifter for your front chain-rings is always on the left, the rear on the right. There are usually two 'paddles' on the shifter: one that you push with your thumb to change into a bigger chain-ring/rear sprocket (bigger on the front makes the going harder, on the rear it makes it easier), and one that you click with the forefinger to change back.

Grips

The 'grips' are the soft, rubber pads that you hold on to. Most mountain bikes are now supplied with 'lock-on' grips, which are held in place by a ring at either end of the grip that tightens with an Allen key. Soft grips are not necessarily more comfortable – many people find their hands fatigue less with firmer ones. Also, note that different width grips are available; most companies offer thin, medium and thick, which are for different hand sizes, so make sure you find a comfortable set.

Brakes

Big advancements in braking technology mean that nearly all quality mountain bikes are now sold with hydraulic disc-brakes, even bikes around the £300 mark. These are far better for stopping than traditional rim-brakes and are less affected by water/mud and buckled wheels; much more useful for mountain biking. All brakes use either synthetic or mineral oil to operate; the oil essentially pushes two pads against the disc, which is attached to the centre of the wheel, to slow you down.

2-pot, 4-pot and 6-pot simply refer to the number of cylinders that push against the back of the brake pad to force it against the disc. In theory, a 6-pot brake should be better, as the extra 'pots' should dissipate heat more efficiently – heat causes many problems on long descents. However, many manufacturers

Handlebar width and stem length can play a huge part in the handling of the bike.

decide that simplicity is best and that one big 'pot' either side of the brake caliper (a 2-pot brake) will deliver sufficient power and cooling qualities.

Wheels

Everyone recognizes a wheel, but it is more difficult to know good quality from poor quality. Most bikes come with machine-built wheels, which, although not built with the same attention to detail as a specific wheel builder (wheel building is considered an art form by some), will most certainly be well-structured and balanced. The problem comes when buying an after-market wheel. As a rule of thumb, do not expect a cheap, fully-built wheel from an internet store to last any more than a week's worth of riding. The process of building a wheel is long and laborious; a process that is cut down to a minimum to lower costs by internet stores. Buy from a local bike shop or, if you do go for the online

bargain, drop it into your local shop for a re-tensioning of the spokes before you even use it.

Tyres

The tyre is another part of the bike that is seemingly self-explanatory, but in actual fact deserves a lot of attention. Cheap tyres (under £20) will look the part but are made from cheap rubber that is plastic in feel and is almost dangerously slippery in use. You also need to be aware of the 'side-wall' quality – literally the side of the tyre, which usually has the manufacturer's mark and the tyre's dimensions printed upon – as thin, almost papery side-walls come on cheaper tyres and lead to many punctures, with the tyre's lifespan being vastly shorter than something above £20.

Tyre width ranges from 1.95in (only for serious cross-country racing) to 2.5in (for downhill use only). For general riding, something between 2in and 2.35in is

Setting-up your bike well will ensure a well-functioning machine.

off. This is taken care of by a certain amount of oil in some shocks, in others it is also 100 per cent down to the compressed air in the shock unit.

Coil sprung means that the rear shock or forks are suspended by a spring – usually made of steel but some prefer lighter but more expensive titanium – and the rebound and damping duties are taken care of by oil flowing through valves and shims within the shock/forks. You can distinguish a coil/oil rear shock, as the spring is on the outside of the shock body. To tell the forks from air forks, look for a valve on the top of the forks – this is where you add air to an air chamber so no valve equals coil sprung.

Set-Up

Stem

The first place to start with setting up any bike is to look at the stem length. It is impossible for a bike manufacturer to provide a stem that will fit every body shape and size, so, assuming that you have the correct frame size, you now need to fit the right stem.

A good gauge of stem length is to be in a seated position with your feet on the pedals (you can lean against a wall to make this easier). If your arms are straight to the handlebar, then the reach is too long and you should try a shorter stem. Equally, if the handlebars feel too close – your arms will be struggling for space in the cockpit area – you can try a longer stem. Remember that your ultimate goal is to be comfortable on the bike.

Stem sizes range from 35mm up to 90mm, but realistically you shouldn't need anything longer than 60mm when mountain biking; any longer and you will struggle with steering around tight turns.

Handlebars

Handlebars vary massively in width, rise and sweep, and it is really a case of finding something that is comfortable for your body size and shape. A common width for

perfect. The narrower the tyre, the less rolling resistance, but wider tyres will find more grip and are more stable, so you must make a decision about which is most important.

Derailleurs

The 'derailleur' is a French word and describes the mechanism that moves the chain through the gears – your bike has a front and rear derailleur. Some people prefer simply to call this the front or rear 'mech'. The rear derailleur is in a vulnerable position on a mountain bike – subject to attack from rocks, tree stumps, etc., so is therefore attached to the frame via a 'mech-hanger' with the intended purpose of breaking before the frame is damaged. Mech-hangers are available from all bike shops but vary from bike to bike.

Chain Device

The chain device is a piece of kit that is essential for downhill bikes but optional for all others. A guide at the top of the chain-ring, and a tensioner at the bottom, ensure the chain does not rattle off the

chain-ring. The guide sits close to the top of the chain-ring, which stops the chain jumping or falling off to either side. The tensioner stops the chain moving away from the chain-ring at the bottom and also puts tension on the chain, taking out some of the slack that leads to the chain falling off in the first place. Plastic bash-guards are also commonplace on bikes with a chain device, and these simply attach to the chain-ring, sitting slightly proud around its circumference and ensuring that rocks and other objects cannot bend or damage the chain-ring.

Different Types of Suspension

There are two ways of suspending a bike: air sprung; and coil sprung.

Air sprung means that there is no physical spring on the suspension unit; instead, air under high pressure and a series of valves take care of supporting your weight. When you ride over a bump, the wheel is displaced and, as the suspension moves into action, the air is compressed. More air pressure in the suspension unit will equate to a firmer, stiffer ride. When the shock rebounds it must be damped – slowed down or controlled – so that you are not thrown handlebars is 720mm – this is wide enough to be stable, yet should fit through gaps on the trail easily enough.

A common error is to have bars that are too wide, as this will affect the bend of your arm and also bring you very far forward on the bike. Some downhill racers use bars up to 780mm wide, but you really have to have the shoulder width to go with them or you will struggle to control your bike.

The height at which you have your handlebars is determined by the stack height of your forks and headset; this means the height of your fork steerer-tube plus the headset (the set of bearings by which the forks are allowed to rotate for steering) and can then be fine-tuned by adding or reducing the number of spacers between the stem and headset.

Try to keep this number to a minimum to keep flex to a minimum and to retain a relatively low centre of gravity.

Tyre Pressures

The air in your tyres is vital to the way that your bike handles – your tyres are your only contact patch with the ground you are riding across after all – and such a simple mistake as incorrect tyre pressure can rule out any other set-up of the components on your bike. Take the time to experiment with tyre pressures but remember that the lower you go, the more grip you will get (as your tyre is more able to deform around ground objects) and the higher pressure, the faster you will roll (as the increasingly

rounded profile of the tyre means less contact with the ground and therefore less resistance.

Shock Pressures

The amount of air in the chamber of your bike's shock unit or suspension forks affects how hard the suspension is and can also affect the action of the suspension. For heavier riders, higher pressures are necessary to support the extra weight, but there is no specific rule for all makes and models. You must refer to the bike or suspension handbooks to find a chart of rider weight to air pressure; this will give you a good base to work from and you can then fine-tune according to personal preference.

Shock pressures are vital but also easily adjusted.

CHAPTER 3

KIT AND EQUIPMENT

Introduction

In mountain biking there is an apparent abundance of kit needed. When thinking of all the variables across the sport, this is unsurprising: changing seasons; changeable weather; varying terrain; different disciplines … the list goes on. Having an understanding of the kit you will need to start out in the sport is important, but remember that aside from a good-quality helmet, you can ride a bike in any kit – the technical fibres and fashionable kits are not vital but will help. Most people don't have an unlimited budget to start out with so build your kit up over time and don't worry, as long as you have a good helmet, you are safe to ride.

Kit and equipment are both plentiful and important in mountain biking.

Technical Clothing

Choosing the right kit for a mountain bike ride can be a confusing series of decisions, often dependant on the season, the weather and of course your own personal preferences. There is a base of kit that you will need on every ride: helmet, gloves and footwear. For differing conditions, the rest of your kit will need to vary and adjust accordingly.

Gloves

Gloves for mountain biking are almost a necessity as they not only stop your hands from becoming sore on long rides, but also prevent minor injuries from falls and scrapes from branches, brambles and so on. A good pair of gloves is worth the investment, as cheaper models will tear with little use. Although half-finger gloves are available, it is best to go for full-finger models for complete protection.

The padding on the palm of gloves ranges in bulk, with most riders preferring little in the way of soft pads; these limit feel and can adjust the position of your hand on the handlebar. However, for those who suffer from quickly fatiguing and cramping hands, gloves with padding targeted at reducing this effect are available (look for Specialized's 'Body Geometry' range).

Choose a glove that your hand is secure in – so that there is no 'scrunching up' on the palm of the glove – and you will limit sores and blisters.

Use: protection of hands and prevention of sore palms.
Price range: £20+.
Top brands: 661, Fox, Specialized.

Jackets

The jacket is an invaluable piece of kit for any mountain biker. In Britain a jacket may be necessary on the majority of rides, but even in good conditions, one should always carry at least a lightweight jacket in a trail-pack, as the weather in any mountainous area is greatly changeable and at altitude, even on a sunny day, you can catch a chill. The jacket is also invaluable in the instance of an injury, as keeping an injury victim warm can not only boost their morale but, in extreme cases, can save their life.

There are a number of textiles that are all developed with the same intention: to

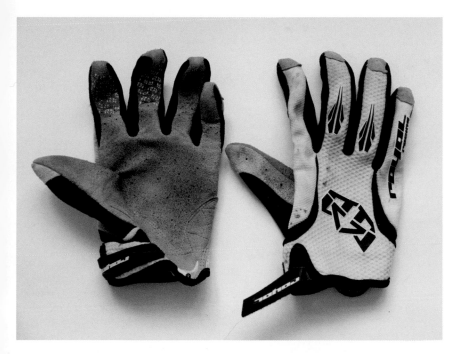

Gloves provide your contact patch with the controls, so it is important to choose the right ones for you.

Shorts

Shorts are a piece of kit that is seemingly straightforward, yet on further inspection you will discover a large range of variables that can make choosing a pair quite difficult. The main differences between various brands and intentions are in the material and padding. Downhill shorts, made almost exclusively of nylon, are thick, heavy and very durable; they are made to cope with falls and to help prevent injury. For trail riding, shorts are developed with the intention of being lightweight and practical, with multiple pockets, venting, sweat-wicking properties and a comfortable fit that is suitable for all-day riding. Cross-country specific shorts are normally made from Lycra, a tight-fitting, sweat-wicking material that is practical in mountain biking only for race events – for everyday riding, a trail short is better suited.

Look for a small zip-pocket on the hip as this can be very useful for storing valuables and items that you need to hand, such as mobile phones, cash and lift passes.

make a waterproof, breathable and lightweight jacket. The names to look for include Gore-Tex, which is one of the most popular and a fabric used by many manufacturers. Fibres that repel water and yet let the jacket breathe from the inside (to prevent the jacket from acting like a big 'boil in a bag') are highly technical and do not come cheaply. Basic jackets, normally made from PVC, are attainable for a much lower price and if you are simply looking for something to carry for emergencies or rain showers, then these will suit.

It is worth buying a cycling specific jacket as they drop lower at the rear than a standard cut – this is so that when in riding position, the jacket doesn't ride up your back exposing it to the elements.

Use: rain storms; emergencies; changing weather and temperature drop.
Price range: technical fabrics £100+; basic jacket £10+.
Top brands: The North Face, Endura, Gore.

A quality jacket comes into use not only when it is raining.

Royal are one of the most popular brands and have a great range of shorts for different rides.

Function: sweat-wick; comfortable fit; venting; pockets including zip-pocket for phone/money, etc.; graze/abrasion prevention.
Price range: £25+.
Top brands: Royal, Oakley, Fox, Endura.

Flats vs SPDs

There are two distinct types of pedal to choose from: flat pedals; and SPDs.

Flat pedals are essentially a platform for your foot to sit on and are normally made from a block of machined metal with 'pins' – a collection of upright metal spikes – to hold your foot in place and prevent slipping. In theory, one can use any footwear whatsoever with a flat pedal and should attain a certain level of grip but mountain bike specific footwear is widely available.

'SPD' is an abbreviation of 'Shimano Pedalling Dynamics' – a marketing tag that has become the common nickname for 'clipless' – without old fashioned toe straps. The SPD is a mechanical pedal that a 'cleat' – a small metal block attached to the under-sole of a specific shoe – clicks into thus holding the foot in place. The foot will not leave the pedal in an upward motion except under extreme pressure. To disengage from an SPD, the rider twists their foot to either side.

Advantages of Flat Pedals

- Easy to mount/dismount. Although you do have to find a comfortable location for your foot when you jump on, this happens instinctively and almost instantly. For learning or practising skills, flats are recommended, as they are far safer and easier to take a foot off from. Some people like to drag a foot when cornering, which makes flats a popular choice for experienced riders.
- Confidence. Flats are confidence-inspiring as you can put your foot on the ground at any moment.
- Comfort. The footwear available is often more comfortable than that on offer for SPDs and the normal shoe styling makes flat pedal footwear

> **TOP TIP**
>
> Although the advantages of SPD pedals sound very inviting, it is highly recommended to start off on flats and, indeed, to do any further learning on them. The reason for this is that flat pedals aid you in developing a good technique for all technical aspects of your riding – SPDs only lead to laziness and therefore poor technique – of course, you'll be able to jump off the bike more easily too. Learn on flat pedals and, when you have conquered the core skills and vitals such as the bunny hop and the wheelie, decide whether you would like to be clipped in.

more agreeable for all-day riding and longer trips.

Advantages of SPDs

- Attached to bike. Many SPD users really like the feeling of being attached to the bike, as it means that the bike will always go where you go, lift up when you lift up and so on. A rider's feet are also unlikely to be rattled loose over extremely rough ground, leaving them free to think about the trail ahead.
- Pedalling efficiency. Nearly all cross-country racers and many enduro and downhill racers use SPDs for their increased pedalling efficiency and the ability to pull up on the pedal, as well as to push down, enables an efficient circular pedalling motion.

Footwear

Choosing the right footwear is one of the most important factors when buying a kit for mountain biking, as your shoes are one of the two contact patches that you have with the bike (the second being your hands). There are two main categories for shoes to fall into: flats and clips (also known by most as SPDs).

Flat Pedal Footwear

In the past, riders wanting to use flat pedals had to derive their shoes from the skateboard industry, but now there are several companies making mountain bike specific shoes.

The intention of a mountain bike shoe is to provide a huge amount of grip to keep the rider's foot on the pedal, and to protect and support the foot. Grip is provided by specially formulated rubbers that were originally developed for the climbing industry. Extremely soft compound rubbers 'stick' the rider's foot to the pedal and the advance in footwear technology has seen a huge rise in the popularity of flat pedal riding.

These shoes are made by Teva and from the new-school of flat-pedal shoes.

SPD Footwear

SPD shoes have been developing ever since the first mountain bike was produced, with products originally being taken from the road cycling industry but soon being adapted for off-road duties. Two styles of SPD shoe are available: a 'slipper-style' shoe that hugs the foot and provides a very rigid platform, which is good for racing as it maximizes efficiency of power-output; and a 'skate-style', which is based on flat-pedal footwear and is a lot easier to walk in – better for all-day and general riding. With the latter, the 'cleat' – the part of the shoe that clicks into the pedal – is sunken into a recess on the sole, which adds comfort.

What to Look For

With both styles of footwear there are several factors to differentiate between their purposes. The level of protection for the foot and ankle should be of most concern to those who ride regularly in mountainous and especially rocky places; good ankle support and protection can prevent many injuries. However, the extra padding around the ankle on a 'boot'-style shoe does have its downsides, particularly in hot weather when it can increase the effect of the heat. Low-cut shoes are more commonly used and preferred, as they aid cooling and many find them to be more comfortable.

Materials are advancing, with industry giants taking an interest in the mountain bike market, and companies such as Teva are now producing highly technical footwear that can boast water-resistant properties, ergonomic fit and durable construction. All qualities to be noted and looked for in any shoe for mountain biking.

Shoes that feel flexible and comfortable when you try them on won't necessarily be good for riding in. A sturdy sole in either a flat or SPD shoe reduces the onset of fatigue and foot cramps that come with long descents.

Function: grip; rigidity; comfort; injury prevention.
Price range: £40+
Top brands: Teva, Five Ten, Shimano.

Base Layers

The layering system is often talked about in the outdoors world – layer up well and you will end up needing to carry far less bulky clothing (as the spaces in-between layers trap air that warms up and retains your body warmth) and you will also be able to lose layers with rising temperatures. The most important layer is at the base: the layer that is against your skin. When clothes are wet they lose up to 90 per cent of their insulting values, and having sweaty layers against your body is one way to commence the onset of hypothermia, so choosing a material that wicks sweat away from the body is of utmost importance.

A good base layer can work equally to keep you cool as it can warm, so look for information on clothes tags as to the intended usage and season for a particular base layer. In warm weather, a lightweight base layer allows air to circulate. Synthetic materials such as nylon and polyester are good for sweat-wicking properties and dry quickly. In cold weather, a warmer material is sensible, the best being merino wool, which is praised for its superior warmth due to air that is trapped amongst the many intricate fibres.

Avoid wearing cotton T-shirts or jerseys as a base layer – these only retain sweat, which will rapidly lead to loss of body heat

Invest in two base layers: one for warm weather and one for cold. When setting out on a ride, choose your base and then layer up so that you start the ride cool; when you start exercising, you will warm up and avoid overheating or excessively sweating.

Rain Kit

Mountain biking, thankfully, is not a seasonally affected sport and one of its attractions is the potential to ride year-round. Although it is occasionally difficult to find the motivation to get out in the elements when it is raining and cold, there are several wet weather essentials that will really help.

Lizard Skins/Waterproof Socks

Having wet feet can hugely affect not only your mood, but also your body temperature, and can lead to problems such as trench foot in the long run. A good pair of waterproof socks (Lizard Skins are the best known brand) can avoid these problems and make your winter riding far more enjoyable.

Waterproof Trousers

A lightweight pair of trousers that can be 'thrown on' over your ordinary riding kit can be easily packed into a trail bag and will not only prevent a soggy bottom, but will mean that your kit is left mud-free with only the trousers needing a quick hose-down after a ride – something that will help you to be motivated to get back out there.

Under-Gloves

Although waterproof gloves are available specifically for bike riding, one of the best tips is to pick up some plastic gloves (such as those found on fuel station forecourts) and to wear them underneath your normal gloves. Dry hands are warm hands and warm hands offer far more control of the bike.

Neoprene Mud Flap

The RRP mud flap attaches via six Velcro straps between the crown and brace of your forks, closing the gap between tyre and crown. This stretchy neoprene flap is brilliant in its simplicity and can fold up very small if you wish to keep it in your backpack when not needed. These are actually far more effective than traditional mud-guards as

A good-quality helmet is the most valuable investment you will make.

they limit the mud that flies from your front tyre upward and forward, and thus into your face as you move forward.

Protective Wear

Although a thoroughly fun sport, which can be approached with any level of enthusiasm, the sport of mountain biking can, at times, be dangerous. In fact, by its very nature the sport can provide numerous potential dangers, whatever speed you ride at. Protective equipment is not an option, it is a necessity.

Essential Protection: Helmet

Helmets are the most necessary of all kit – never ride off-road without a helmet. Although many people ride on tarmac without a helmet – a move that is putting oneself at unnecessary risk – it is important to remember that you are far more likely to have a tumble on a mountain bike and, even at low speed, one mistake could prove disastrous. Whenever buying a new helmet, be sure to take your time to choose something that is not only physically comfortable, but that you will be happy wearing at all times when out on your bike.

Safety Standards
Does it conform to European and British standards? All helmets sold in bike shops should do, but look out for the stickers to be sure.

Is it Designed for the Right Purpose?
Mountain bike helmets have a lot of venting, 'in-moulded' shells (the plastic shell is effectively part of the polystyrene structure, not just taped or glued in place), easily adjustable fittings for all head shapes and plenty of ventilation.

Level of Protection
For racing, some people prefer a helmet with an open rear section for increased cooling and heat loss, but for general day-to-day riding, you should be looking for a helmet that offers a good level of protection to all areas, including reaching down the back of your head.

Comfort
The last thing you want is to be distracted from your riding by uncomfortable headgear, so be sure to try the helmet on for longer than a quick size-check. You will be wearing it at all times, so it pays to be patient when making the purchase.

Shop Not Internet
Although some internet sites boast lower prices than high-street shops, there is usually a reason. Some of those reasons include a lack of packaging, which can lead to damaged goods, and out-of-date stock. The main reason to visit a store, however, is for the fitting service, advice and after-sales service that you won't get with online shopping. The last thing you want is to be stuck with a wrongly fitting helmet.

Knee Pads

Knee pads come in all shapes and sizes: some extending to cover the shin; some with a hinged metal structure; and some with minimal yet effective padding. Although not favoured by cross-country riders, almost all downhillers wear knee pads at all times, and the majority of trail riders will wear them for at least the descents. Knee pads do make your legs hot, but it will be worth it for the prevented injuries – even a slip of the chain can mean that you bang your knee on the handlebar, which could potentially put you out of action.

Well-constructed knee pads will nearly always have a thick layer of foam padding with a plastic shell to deflect stones, prevent abrasions and so on. The foam padding should wrap around the knee to provide adequate protection for the important ACL and MCL ligaments that are on the side of the patella (knee cap). Some pads have a thicker plastic cup for the knee to sit in that prevents intrusion by sharp rocks and objects.

Knee pads are comfy and lightweight, and they are worn by the majority of riders for all descending.

Knee-Pad Materials
'Smart', high-density impact resistant foams are being used by manufacturers in a range of padding, tagged 'D3O' by its most prolific user: 661. This material is supple enough to deform around your knee, yet with a sharp impact it changes state and toughens to almost solid. This can be ideal for trail riders who want the highest level of comfort and flexibility for long rides without sparing protection. However, some think that sharp, pointed objects will not be protected against by the 'smart pads', and they come with a much higher price tag.

Elbow Pads

Much like knee pads, elbow pads are usually a simple construction of soft but resilient foam padding combined with a plastic outer shell. Less preferred by the majority, elbow pads can be seen as

Sunglasses will suffice but specific bike glasses are available and goggles are preferred by most gravity riders.

problematic, as they often slip down the arm whilst riding. However, some designs do work to stay in place and the benefits of protecting one's elbows need not be explained.

Body Armour

Full body armour provides padding for most areas of the upper body, including the spine and rib-cage, as well as a kidney-belt and integrated shoulder and elbow pads. It is important to note that body armour will not prevent injury, only limit it. Although sometimes very hot to wear, body armour is a wise choice, especially if

you intend on trying some downhill or uplift-aided riding.

Look for well-articulated joints, plenty of venting, especially around the arm-pit, and a sturdy back-plate. Most models of body armour come with a detachable back-plate, which is helpful if you are riding something less extreme but still wish to have elbow and shoulder protection. As with helmets, sizing is vital, so make sure that armour fits comfortably and doesn't move around too much. As a note, it is always a good idea to wear a light base layer underneath your armour to prevent chaffing and to limit odour. Wash armour regularly, as it can quickly pick up a pong.

Eye Protection

Any conditions when out mountain biking can call for eye protection for a number of preventative reasons: to keep mud, rain, sticks, stones, dust and more out of your eyes; to counteract the effects of sunlight through tinted lenses; and to limit the airflow to your eyes, which can make your eyes water. All of which will increase your concentration levels.

Goggles are more commonly used with full-face helmets and are the most practical eye-wear. Goggles have a wrap-around shape, a large range of vision, they stay in place thanks to adjustable elasticated straps, eradicate the possibility of mud entering the eye and have easily interchangeable lenses. Sunglasses are more popular with trail riders and suit open-faced helmets better than goggles. Look for a pair that has three interchangeable lenses: tinted; clear; and light-enhancing (usually yellow).

Backpacks

The backpack is as much an essential piece of kit as the bike itself: ride without at least one amongst a group and you will soon be in trouble. As a method to carry everything from food to first aid, a quality pack is worth purchasing.

There are varying sizes of pack and the most avid of mountain bikers tend to have more than one size for differing ride

TOP TIP

As a lot of riding is subject to changeable weather and rain storms, you want to keep the contents of your trail pack dry. There are several solutions to this: one is the removable rain cover that some bags come with as standard, although these do have a tendency to get lost or pulled off the bag in high winds. The other option is to keep your kit dry from the inside, by putting everything into a dry-bag. These are simply a waterproof pack with a fully sealed opening at the top and are 100% waterproof, but cost upward of £15. The cheaper alternative is to simply use a bin bag for the main contents and then to individually place your valuables, and most importantly your map, into zip-loc freezer bags, which are fully sealable yet cost next to nothing.

lengths (as you won't need to carry as much water, food and spares if you are only a short distance from your starting point). Try to look for a pack that has as many features and separate storage pockets as possible, in order to separate your food and water from your spares.

Backpack Features

- *Capacity:* a good size pack is around 14ltr storage space.
- *Hydration:* the pack should come with a hydration bladder or at least the separate storage space and appropriate routing for the hose. A 3ltr bladder is large but you don't have to fill it to the top if you don't want to carry the weight.

Osprey make some of the toughest and best thought-out back-packs.

- *Rain cover:* separate rain covers come as standard with many packs and if not, can be purchased cheaply and stored in a small space.
- *Straps:* comfortable hip and chest straps are vital and you must check that they do the job of keeping the pack in place for your body shape – when riding you don't want the pack lurching up and interfering with your helmet.
- *Additional protection:* some bike-specific packs feature optional spine protection – a great and simple idea and ideal for trail riders.
- *Reflective strips:* night riding, and indeed any riding near or on roads, will be a lot safer if you are highly visible.

- *Helmet attachment:* on long climbs or transfers you may want to attach your helmet to the outside of your backpack; this has been tackled in a number of ways by different manufacturers with the most effective system being that of Osprey – a simple elasticated stretch cord with a rubber fitting that sits in one of your helmet's vents.

Trail Pack Contents

On nearly every mountain bike ride, however far away or close to home, at least one member of a group is going to need to carry a backpack. With all the rocks, mud and obstacles encountered on any ride into the mountains or forest comes breakages, punctures and occasionally injuries. It is sensible to have a well-stocked trail bag at the ready containing essentials and spares that include the following:

- *First-aid kit:* including plasters, bandages, triangular bandages, antiseptic wipes/fluid.
- *Inner tubes:* always carry at least one Presta-valved tube, as the thin valves will fit any rim.
- *Puncture repair kit:* modern fast adhesion patch kits work well and are far more user-friendly than the old glue and patch kits.

A well-stocked backpack is essential.

- *Multi-tool:* a quality multi-tool should include a range of Allen-key sizes, chain tool and Torx tool.
- *Tyre levers:* for tricky-to-get-off tyres.
- *Jacket:* for rain storms and injury victims.
- *High-energy snacks:* such as energy bars and gels, not only to get you home but also to help any other member of the group suffering exhaustion, dehydration or cramping.
- *Water:* not only to drink, but also to wash out any cuts and grazes.
- *Pliers:* for any fixes or trail-side bodges.
- *Knife.*
- *Spare gloves:* keep these in a dry bag, they can boost morale and importantly help to prevent hypothermia in an injury victim.
- *Mobile phone:* for emergencies.
- *Spoke key:* as a bent wheel can make the difference between making it home and staying on a mountain side.
- *Map:* of the area where you are riding (it is also a good idea to plan and mark variations to your route on the map in case your original ride length proves too ambitious).
- *Pump:* any mini-pump is suitable, but the best have a lever that you can stand on and therefore pump as you would with a track pump at home – this saves a huge amount of energy.
- *Suspension/shock pump:* not necessary, but a good idea to carry at least one amongst a group.
- *Emergency blanket:* a silver-foil blanket is not only for those who are injured,

but also vital if you are lost, caught in a rain storm or suffer a mechanical failure and must wait to be rescued.
- *Small essentials:* zip ties, insulating tape, Velcro strips, spare change.

Remember that the more you pack into your bag, the heavier the load on your bike. Therefore, be sure to check your suspension set-up with your pack and full kit on, and adjust air pressure accordingly.

Global Positioning System (GPS)

GPS has reached mountain biking and is now one of the most useful pieces of modern technology to the avid explorer. There are two main functions of GPS: navigation and fitness tools. The GPS market is large and ever-expanding, with the leader in the field being Garmin, whose units are robust, reliable and user-friendly. However, even with proven brand names, it is still important to understand where you are putting your money, so read the following outlines of the two functions and then follow the feature guidelines below:

Navigation

In order to navigate successfully from a portable GPS unit, you need to be sure that you can upload and view detailed maps and that you aren't going to be limited to basic road mapping. You will also need a colour screen in order to view and differentiate between the features on a detailed ordinance map. These detailed maps take up a lot of memory space, so be sure that an external memory card slot is present.

Navigation Uses
- Upload and track your rides.
- Mark points of interest.
- Log your statistics such as average speed, elevation, top speed and ride distance.

Digital navigation can be very helpful but must not be fully relied upon.

- A good GPS unit will guide you back to your route if you get off track.

Fitness

Many GPS units also boasts fitness software and can connect to heart-rate monitors, which, when combined with the ability to log your ride length, proves the most effective way of tracking your fitness routine. Make sure that you can connect to a heart-rate monitor and if this is your main intention when purchasing a GPS, then consider the more expensive models that boast wireless connection and integrated heart-rate monitor, pre-set fitness plans, and suchlike.

Fitness Uses
- Log and track your energy output.
- Time and compare regular rides.
- Find average speeds, power output and so on.

TOP TIP

Be sure to study the feature list of any GPS thoroughly, as many cheaper models have short battery life and lack important features, such as an external memory card. Good GPS units are not cheap but it is worth investing in the higher priced models to ensure accuracy and consistent satellite coverage.

PART 2

SKILLS AND TECHNIQUES

CHAPTER 4

CORE SKILLS

Introduction

The set of skills needed to deal with the variable conditions that mountain biking can offer is as broad and diverse as the sport itself. However, you must learn the fundamentals before attempting any specific trail skills.

In this chapter you will find a description of the essentials, starting with a good body position and moving on to four elementary lessons that you can learn and then continue to practise throughout your riding career.

Body Position

Without a good position on the bike you can't begin to build your skills; you need a good base to work from – solid foundations. Your position on the bike ultimately determines how your weight is distributed between the wheels, and shifting your weight fore and aft will alter how much grip your tyres achieve. It is important to start with a good, central body position on your bike that will be both comfortable and effective.

Step 1: Good Cock-Pit Set-Up for a Good Riding Position

The first step to a good riding position is to start with your machine and to make sure that it isn't going to hinder your progress. Many mistakes in set-up can be made and they can just as easily be corrected. Brake lever position, handlebar tilt and height and stem length are all factors in making a good, or very bad, set-up choice.

Be sure to refer to Chapter 2 before

Core skills improve your entire ride.

Good body position on the bike will let you attack the trails with confidence.

working on your skills – good overall bike set-up is vital if you wish to improve.

Step 2: Heels and Wrists

'Dipping' your heels will help you to control the bike, reduce fatigue and to become more stable when descending or riding technical sections.

When in standing position, simply push your heels towards the floor so that your toes are pointing slightly upward. You will now have a stable pedal platform to push against when encountering obstacles and your feet won't be shaken off the pedals!

A similar rule applies to your wrists, as keeping a straight line from shoulder to brake lever will make it difficult to keep your grip and control your bike. Roll your hands backward slightly so that there is a slight bend in the wrist. If you are now

Dipping your heels and wrists will help you to find a stable standing position.

A good, central body position will distribute your weight effectively.

struggling to reach your brake levers comfortably, simply roll them 'upward' – toward horizontal – until you are comfortable.

Step 3: Centralize

It is important to have grip through the tyres – a statement that seems obvious – but how to regulate and enhance grip? And where does the grip come from?

In order for your tyres to 'dig' into the ground – to find grip – they need weight on them. The main weight available to them is from you, the rider; therefore, it is down to you to move your weight into position for your tyres to be weighted and finding grip.

You clearly want grip on both wheels, so a good place to start is to look at an 'ideal' riding position: Stand up on your

bike (perhaps try this whilst leant against a wall to make things easier), with your heels and wrists dipped, looking up and ahead. You are looking for a central position over the bike; a good rule of

PROBLEM SOLVING

If you think that your weight is too far back, perhaps your bars are rolled back too far in the stem? The rearward curve of all handlebars naturally brings you fore/aft on the bike, depending on how much you roll the bars in the stem.
If you think that you are too far forward, rolling the handlebars toward the seat will bring your weight further back. You also may have your stem too low, which is easily adjusted by moving one or two of the spacers from above it and putting them below.

thumb is that your head should be above or beyond the handlebars and your bum above the saddle.

If you aren't in this position, or are struggling to comfortably stay like it, then you need to adjust the bike's set-up; your body shape can't be changed. Try rolling the handlebars, adjusting handlebar height, changing brake lever tilt and different stem lengths. This may take some time but you'll only have to do it once and your riding will benefit greatly.

Core Skill: Climbing

With all disciplines throughout the sport, you will come across the same varying, undulating terrain that makes it important to be able to adapt your body position quickly and naturally, with minimal effort. Changing your position on the bike should be instinctive and intuitive, but when learning it is helpful to follow a set of rules that will make your ride a lot simpler.

When climbing, there are a number of steps to take that are as follows:

Step 1: The Approach

As you approach you should assess, choose your gear and carry your speed into the climb. Think about how long/ steep the climb is and choose a sensible gear accordingly. You should have a steady cadence (the speed that your cranks are turning) that is reasonably easy to push. You don't want your legs to be spinning furiously, and likewise you don't want to be putting a lot of pressure through the pedals – you'll tire quickly in either of these scenarios.

You should aim to be seated on the climb, as this will save you valuable energy and will automatically put your weight slightly rearward thus giving the drive wheel more traction.

Step 2: Elbows In, Front Wheel Down

An easy way to obtain a good climbing position is to tuck your elbows in slightly. Tucking in will bring your weight down, putting further grip on to the tyres and also give you an 'attacking' position, which will help you to put power into the pedals.

You want to have your weight down as much as possible, as this will stop the front wheel lifting on steeper sections of the climb.

Step 3: Gear Changes

Clearly every hill isn't going to be a constant gradient from start to finish, so you may need to change your gear accordingly. If you are tiring, then you might need to move into an easier gear too! This sounds simple, but as there is a lot of power going through the drive-train whilst climbing, you need to be careful not to force through the gears.

As you change gear, ease your pedalling slightly and move through the gears

On this short, steep climb, elbows tucked in and head down helps keep the front wheel on the ground.

Steady pedalling ensures grip to the rear wheel.

one-by-one rather than forcing the gear shifter – the components of your expensive bike will last a lot longer.

Step 4: Steady Body

Climbing is naturally one of the most physically demanding parts of mountain biking, so you want to make things as easy as possible. Jerking on the handlebars, thrashing from side to side, and puffing and panting can all start to happen when you tire, but none are going to help you get up the hill.

Try and stay seated with a stable upper torso, eyes focused on the trail and keep your head steady. Think about putting all your power into your spinning legs instead of any upper-body swaying and your drive will come from your hips downward.

Core strength is important when climbing, as you need it to stabilize your body and focus your power to your legs, so think about some core stability training.

Training. Core strength, stamina, quads and calf muscles are all key to climbing.

Climbing Components

- SPD pedals may help you to spin your legs whilst climbing and to obtain a more efficient drive from your pedals, as you can 'pull up' on the pedals on the up-stroke. Think about the amount of climbing and easy trail-riding you aim to do, compared with technical and steeper riding, and decide whether you think SPD pedals could serve as an advantage to you.

PROBLEM SOLVING

If your front wheel is continuously wanting to lift off the ground, try to really pull your elbows in towards each other as this naturally moves you forward. If you are still struggling then you could have a stem that is too short, your seat too far back on the seat rails or your bike could be too small for you.

If you are struggling to gain traction, then you either need to lower your cadence (the speed your feet are spinning) by moving up a gear, just as you would in a car on slippery ground, or you need to transfer more weight to the rear. Assuming you are seated, your weight is already being transferred to the rear wheel effectively, however you can move the seat backward a little on the seat rails to bring your weight further rear.

Lowering the pressure of your rear tyre will help the tyre to deform around obstacles on the ground, gaining larger surface area and therefore more grip. If you try this approach then take care not to lower pressure too much or you will risk punctures.

The downhills are the reason that you climbed to the top!

- Gravity dropper seat-posts are a relatively new technology in mountain biking, but are a very worthwhile investment if you intend on riding varied terrain, and especially if the majority of your riding is on very undulating ground. Most dropper posts have a remote switch on the handlebars that you press to either drop or extend the seat-post. The clear advantage of this is that your seat will be instantly out of the way for tricky downhills or straight back to pedalling height for the next up.

Core Skill: Descending

Descending is possibly the most important skill to master in mountain biking as it will provide the most fun! Watch any downhill race and the pros will

Good body position is vital for descending.

make it look incredibly easy – attacking body position, off the brakes and even sprinting down impossibly steep tracks. However, as many mountain bikers find, it really isn't as easy as it looks.

Descending takes skill, nerve and experience, but with the following steps you can settle into an effective position and descending style from which to improve and expand your ability.

Step 1: Body Position

Common sense in mountain biking says to move your weight back on the bike when downhilling, as this will, presumably, stop you from being pitched over the handlebars. However, most people make the mistake of hovering very far back, which actually creates more problems than it solves. Being too far back on the bike will take all weight off the front wheel, making braking ineffective and cornering difficult, as there is no traction for the front tyre.

The best way to descend is to always stand – being seated whilst descending is both uncomfortable and dangerous. Your legs should be reasonably straight (another common misconception is that your legs should be bent to absorb impacts, in fact bending your legs a lot leaves you struggling to support your body weight and also is very unstable on the bike). Therefore, dip your heels, legs straight but not locked out, and you will have a strong, stable, position from which to work.

Step 2: Look Ahead

It sounds incredibly obvious, but most people don't look far enough ahead and instead focus on the patch of ground in front of their wheel. This leaves you to encounter obstacles and corners at the last minute.

You should be reading the terrain that is approaching, not the terrain that you are on. How far ahead you are looking depends on your speed, but the minimum is around 3m in front of your wheel. At first you may find it hard to always look up and ahead, but with very little practise you will find yourself reading what is coming up, setting yourself up for it and instinctively riding the obstacle or corner, whilst looking to the next one.

You should be looking down the trail, not at your front wheel.

Pedals level for downhills.

Step 3: Gauge Your Speed

In a perfect environment, rough ground and corners would be tackled completely off the brakes, the reason being that braking causes your wheels to lock up over rough terrain, your suspension will struggle to react and as you attempt to corner, the forces of braking against the gyroscopic effect of your wheels will be naturally pulling you upright. However, as most mountain bike terrain covers steep hillsides and features that must be tackled at varying speeds, it is important to be in full control of your bike and its speed at all times.

The starting point for efficient descending is to be at a speed that you are completely comfortable with and at which you are able to react to features and obstacles. Therefore, using both brakes a little to calm your speed is not a bad thing. As you progress you will be able to use them less and less, eventually you will find safe 'braking points' – but to begin you should be covering your brake levers, applying each brake lightly and equally so that there is no wheel lock up, and from there you can adjust your rolling speed.

Step 4: Pedals Level

When you are in your basic descending position, your pedals/cranks should always be level (a 3 o'clock/9 o'clock position). This sounds obvious at first – it'll mean you are less likely to scrape/hit your feet on ground obstacles and you will be as stable as possible – but a surprising number of people forget to do this.

As you tire on longer downhills, you may find yourself more prone to dropping a foot to rest, but don't! It is dangerous and unstable – if you are really tired, then stop for a breather.

Step 5: Elbows Out

Much the opposite to climbing, for the downhills you need your full strength from all areas of your body – you need a good 'brace' position from which to absorb impacts and to hold your body stable.

When standing, your elbows should be bent at a comfortable angle – no

---

TOP TIP

Even experienced mountain bikers often overlook seat height as being a major hindrance when descending. Riding with your seat high reduces your clearance of the bike and also the amount you can move your body to react to steeper terrain. Simply lower your seat to a height that is completely out of the way of your legs or bum and you will find every steep section far less daunting.

90-degree bend, but similarly your arms should not be stretched to near straight. Look to have the majority of your weight supported through your feet and legs, with only around 25 per cent of weight through your arms.

Training. Work on your upper-body strength and use the arm-pump exercises.

Core Skill: Cornering

Corners, twists and turns occur on all-mountain bike trails and especially on single-track trails – mountain bikers' favourites. Corners are incredibly difficult to master, as there are so many variables, including changing ground conditions, pitch of terrain and obstacles to avoid. Even seasoned professionals practise their cornering regularly, as it is a skill that can always be improved upon.

However, there is a simple set of rules to follow that are easy to grasp and that will make your bike riding far easier and more efficient in no time.

Step 1: The Approach

As you approach a corner, you should be looking ahead to see where the trail is

Good cornering will help your flow.

The approach.

PROBLEM SOLVING

If you are finding that you are struggling to hold on when on longer downhills – your arms and/or hands are sore and even cramping – there are several ways to lower fatigue, but unfortunately not eliminate it. One common cause of 'arm pump' is that the brake levers are rolled too far towards a vertical position – this means that you must be stretching your reach to pull the lever and your arms will suffer as a result. Try moving the levers to a slightly more horizontal position and this will actually relieve stress on your hands whilst braking.

Everyone's hands are different shapes and sizes, and for this reason manufacturers produce handlebar grips of varying shapes to suit. Often the problem of sore hands can stem from having grips that are too thin, so try replacing yours with something a little fatter. If you have grips that are too fat for your hands, then you will also struggle to hold on to the handlebars and the stress will quickly tire your forearms. A little experimentation is required here!

Finally, you shouldn't be leaning on the handlebars when riding – they are there to control the bike but not to support your full weight – therefore, if you feel that you are really having to hold yourself up through your arms, you are probably too far forward on the bike. This can be changed by moving your handlebars higher (by swapping the stem spacers around), exchanging the handlebars for a version with more upward rise or simply by rolling them backward slightly in the stem.

leading and you should be standing in the level footed position, heels dipped and elbows out. Cover the brakes and bring your speed to a comfortable level – you can quickly get back up to speed out of the turn, so no need to worry about losing your flow.

Step 2: Spy Your Line

Every turn has a 'perfect' line through. Clearly, with the changing rugged terrain that you will encounter when mountain biking, you are not always going to be able to ride this perfect line but you should try to follow this rule: Wide in, apex and wide out. This means that you should enter the turn on a wide line, as far away from the turn as possible. Next, you need to find the 'apex' of the turn – the middle point. From the middle point of the turn you can look for an exit spot – a wide exit point will give you the smoothest, most efficient, arc through the turn.

Step 3: Braking

Ideally you should be completely off the brakes when cornering, as the effects of using your brakes will slow the rotation of the wheels causing stability problems. When your wheels are free to spin, you will also obtain far more grip; if they begin to slide, then as the tyre treads rotate, the fresh treads will dig into the ground, thus regaining grip.

It is tricky to train yourself to let go of the brakes for corners as you are descending, so you should try to practise on a gentle slope first. As with line choice, there is a three-step process to follow: brake in, turn, accelerate out. You can

TOP: *This is a good line; wide in, looking to the apex and wide exit.*

MIDDLE: *Try not to brake once in the corner.*

BOTTOM: *Note how the outside foot is dropped for this fast corner.*

literally be at walking pace on the entry to the turn, as you will soon make your speed back up. Let go of the brakes as you turn and flow out to your exit point.

Step 4: Foot Position

As you reach the apex of your turn, you may find your outside foot dropping; if you are turning right, this means that your left foot will be in the 6 o'clock position, and vice-versa. This is not a problem, in fact as you progress and start to lean your bike into the corners, this will always happen and will help to force grip – your body weight – on to the tyre treads.

However, you should not drop your foot to this position when you are first learning, but instead let it happen naturally. The reason that you should let this happen as a natural progression is that you only need to have your foot dropped when you are really leaning the bike into a turn – for grip and to bring the bike back upright as you exit. Dropping your foot without being leant over will have no positive effect and may cause clearance problems.

Your inside foot should never be dropped whilst cornering – this is both dangerous and ineffective.

Step 5: Exit

As soon as you are out of the corner, you can control your speed and look to the next feature.

PROBLEM SOLVING

If you find yourself consistently missing the exit of the corner and riding into the foliage, then there is either a problem with your technique or you are simply going too fast. Riding really fast on the approach of a corner doesn't always mean that you exit with speed, and more often than not, will ruin your flow as you struggle to slow down.

If you are sure that you are in control of your speed, review the earlier lessons. Perhaps you are looking at your front wheel instead of up and out of the corner – look where you want to go and you will.

As you exit you can build, or lose some speed.

Most good bike riders practise their cornering religiously, as corners are where all the action happens on a trail. If you can corner well, then you can flow through any trail effortlessly. The best place to practise, surprisingly, is in a flat area with some gravel.

Practise turning one way then the other, with feet level, until you feel your tyres beginning to lose traction. If you have a good, central body position, then both tyres will lose traction at the same time. However, this takes a lot of practise to achieve; normally novices find their front wheel losing traction before the rear. Keep practising these flat turns – even 5 minutes of practise before each ride will boost your ability hugely.

ABOVE: Braking must be in control.

Training. Balance skills will help you to understand the forces involved with cornering, so practise on a balance board as much as possible.

Products. The easiest and by far the quickest way to improve your cornering is to change your tyres – they are your contact patch with the terrain you are riding over, so differing tread patterns can make a vast difference to the level of grip achieved. Look for a tyre with side-knobs that are prominent and aggressively patterned; clean, sharp edges that will cut in to the earth. Anything with rounded edges or very low side-knobs is worth avoiding.

Core Skill: Braking

The way that you control your brakes is more important in mountain biking than perhaps any other skill. When mountain biking, one is constantly battling with gravity and changing ground conditions; both making it vital to understand the effects of braking and to control your speed constantly.

RIGHT: Both brakes are in use to control speed.

Hydraulic disc-brakes will stop you in a matter of metres.

Step 1: Basic Braking

Your first step is to learn how to brake.
Use only one or two fingers on the brake lever (with any modern disc or hydraulic brakes, one finger should suffice), so that you still have a good grip on the handle bars. Stand in your 'brace' position with heels and wrists dipped, elbows out and looking ahead. With this confident, strong and composed stance, you will save a lot of energy and hopefully never struggle to lose speed when you need to.

Step 2: Brake to Control

The brakes are not only there to stop you, but also to control your speed. You must learn to use both brakes equally and effectively to limit your speed whilst descending or approaching obstacles without losing traction on the tyres. Find a gentle slope to practise and use both brakes at the same time, but only a little, and vary your speed to find out how much force you need on the brakes.

Step 3: Brake to Stop

The next step is to learn at what point your brakes will stop you and how close to this limit you want to use them. Find a flat area with soft ground – ideally grass – and pedal up to a comfortable rolling speed, then brake until you come to a stop. At first you should not brake too hard – you don't want to be thrown off the bike – but repeat this as many times as you like until you are coming to a stop in a short distance.

Step 4: Front/Rear Specific Braking

With experience, you can use your brakes independently as the easiest and most effective way of controlling your bike whilst descending; a little rear brake can often help to turn the bike, a little front brake can weight the front tyre into a point and lock-up or skid. Whilst out on the trail, skidding is to be avoided, as it will not only wear out your tyre but also hamper your control of the bike. Practise coming to a stop as quickly as possible without skidding and this should become natural whilst out on the trail.

Training. Upper-body exercises and the hand-pump eliminator will help with your braking performance on longer downhills.

Products. Hydraulic disc brakes are commonplace now in mountain biking, even the lowest spec bikes should be equipped with them as standard. To increase power to your discs, you can alter the diameter of the disc – the biggest you can go is 205mm and these are really only for serious downhill riding and racing. A sensible size for all-round riding is 185mm – you will get plenty of power and the large circumference creates more area for heat dissipation under prolonged use.

corner and so on. First though, you need to understand how each brake can have an effect on your ride.

- *Front brake:* on soft, flat ground, ride along at a slow speed and have your weight as far back over the rear wheel as possible. Now pull only the front brake (lightly!) until you come to a stop. Repeat this process until you can feel your weight being pitched forward slightly – go beyond this point and you will be over the handlebars, so be careful. Keep practising this; control of the front brake is one of the most important skills to master.
- *Rear brake:* ride at a medium pace – not so fast that you are likely to lose control – then pull the rear brake until you come to a stop, and repeat. Your rear tyre will lose traction at some

Tyres should have quality rubber and pronounced side and centre knobs for grip.

CHAPTER 5

FURTHER SKILLS

Introduction

Once you have grasped the basics –
you're confident on the descents and
flowing round the corners – it's time to
move on to some more specific skills.
Covered in this chapter are a set of
further skills that will help you through a
range of common features found on
mountain bike trails.

Further Skill: Switch-Back Corners

Turns on the trail come in all shapes and
sizes; flat, banked, off camber, etc., but by
far the trickiest to master is the switch-
back. These feature a lot on natural trails
and are often included in trail-centre
rides. A switch-back is essentially a tight
180-degree flat (i.e. not bermed/banked)
corner. In addition, these can drop steeply
as they turn. A lot of people really
struggle with these, but there are some
simple rules that make switch-backs
relatively easy.

Step 1: The Approach

Switch-backs are the most important
corners to regulate your speed as you
approach. Slow almost to a walking pace if
you like – getting to the apex of the
switch-back with too much speed is not a
good idea.

*OPPOSITE: Further skills are both
fun and useful.*

The approach; look for the line and keep your speed to a minimum.

This is the point of no return; time to commit.

Don't let your attention waver. Focus on the task in hand and try to forget about the potential problems – these are far more likely to occur if you are thinking about them.

The turn.

Make sure you set-up as far to the outside of the entry as possible (i.e. as far to the right as you approach a left-turning switch-back and vice-versa); you'll need every inch of the trail to help you get round the turn. Approach with your pedals level and looking into the mid-point of the turn.

So:

- Slow approach speed.
- Enter corner on the outside line.
- Pedals level.

Step 2: Commitments

As switch-backs often drop steeply and

sometimes give you a nice view over the edge of the hill, they can be nerve-racking and difficult to keep your composure. It is vitally important to keep your cool though, as a panic mid-corner can completely ruin your chances of making it round.

Step 3: The Turn

As you get to the turning point, look round to the exit and keep focused on your actions. Your feet should still be level and you should be keeping your speed under control. As you round the corner, you might find your outside foot (right foot on left-hand corners and vice-versa) wanting to drop; this is fine and will

As you exit, look ahead and assess the approaching terrain.

When you encounter roots, remain calm.

Choose your line wisely.

probably happen quite naturally on these tighter turns.

Step 4: Braking

Braking in corners is never ideal; however, on switch-backs it is often tricky to let go of the brakes fully, as the terrain is usually dropping steeply. This is where a little exception to the rule comes in; relying on the front brake in a switch-back is not the best idea as your weight will likely be far back on the bike and therefore there will be no grip available to the front wheel. (You also don't want to be pitched over the front in this situation.) If you need to use the rear brake heavily, then do so.

Step 5: The Exit

As you pass the mid-point of the corner, you can now look ahead to the trail in front of you. If you see clear trail ahead, let go of the brakes and get back up to rolling speed ready for the next feature.

Further Skill: Tree Roots

Tree roots are to be found on pretty much every UK mountain bike ride; the majority of our bike riding is in forests and even rides that aren't tree-covered are likely to have at least one woodland section. A sprawl of tree roots covering a segment of trail can be incredibly

intimidating, especially when they are wet. There's nothing worse than a shiny, muddy root facing you and causing panic, so it's best to be calm.

Step 1: The Encounter

The most important factor when encountering a rooty section is to be confident. When you spy a section of roots, you should always try to regulate your speed before you enter the section. Your speed over roots doesn't matter – there is no 'too fast' or 'too slow' – pick a speed that you are comfortable with and stick to it, for once you start on the roots, you can't slow down.

Step 2: Keep it Rolling

As with cornering, in order to keep optimum grip through rooty sections of trail, you do not want to be using your brakes (remember that rolling wheels find themselves grip, whereas wheels with braking forces induced will struggle and 'snap out' from under you).

Hopefully you are already at a good speed and as you begin to encounter the roots, let go completely of the brakes (if possible). Your rolling tyres will find the grippy mud in-between the roots, so don't panic if you feel your tyres sliding a little.

Step 3: Line Choice

Naturally, roots will 'sprawl' out from the trees and cover a large area of the ground; the further from the tree, the wider the area that they cover. Therefore, with clever line-choice you can make things a lot simpler for yourself.

If you stop and look at the section of trail, you will note that there are barely any exposed roots close to the tree; this is the same on every technical rooty section you will encounter. So the line choice is simple: ride close to the tree and you will make things a lot easier for yourself.

Step 4: Keep Focused

As already mentioned, confidence is key when riding rooty sections. You must not lose your nerve or panic. Your wheels are likely to be slipping and sliding a little but keep focused on the trail ahead and the next feature or line choice that needs to be made. You will be over the roots before you know it.

Step 5: The Exit

You've modulated your speed, picked a sensible line with the least roots, ridden confidently without braking and now you are leaving the section. Look ahead; there will no doubt be another tree-load of roots and more after that. Pick your lines

ABOVE: *Braking on roots will make your tyres slide-out.*

RIGHT: *These mud tyres have aggressive tread pattern that helps find grip amongst rooty sections.*

PROBLEM SOLVING

Muddy, wet and boggy trail conditions are certainly not unheard of in the UK; in fact they are commonplace. Mud-infested trails will normally cover tree roots that are lurking below the surface ready to catch any unsuspecting rider out. Think sensibly and make an effort to head for the high-points near to trees – as per before, these will hide the least roots. When it is really muddy and slippery on the roots, it is most important not to brake, as your wheels will slip very suddenly.

As you'll almost definitely be travelling at a lower speed, you shouldn't need to slow down too much; just look ahead and remain confident. This takes some experience to get used to but in reality tree roots are not difficult to negotiate.

from tree to tree and try not to spend too much time looking at the ground; this won't help in the slightest, as you already know that the least roots are near to the trees.

You've ridden with confidence and now you are set for sections that will appear on nearly every mountain bike ride in the future.

Training. Tree roots are tough on the arms, so upper-body strength is important.
Products. Tyres are the most important part of your bike with regards to tackling rooty sections. A good tyre for roots needs to find the grippy spaces between the slippery roots. Therefore, you should be looking for something with a deep, widely spaced, tread.

Further Skill: Rocks and Rocky Sections

Rocky sections of trail are commonly found on well-used natural paths, but are also widely used in man-made trail-centres to provide a stable, erosion-free surface. Rocky sections come in all shapes and sizes: there are slabs, paving, slate, wet/dry sections to name a few. Although the appearance of these sections varies, they are all to be tackled in a similar fashion.

Step 1: Assess

As you spot the approaching section of rocks, you'll need to decide on a sensible speed. With most rocky sections, you

Most trails encounter rocky sections at some point.

Choose the right line as you approach.

can't really go too fast; the top speed is dictated only by your confidence and ability. Rolling speed will also help you to 'skim' over the tops of the rocks. Be sensible though – rocks don't move, so you don't want to fall on them.

Step 2: Line Choice

Rocky sections will generally have big holes in-between each rock; these you clearly want to avoid if possible, but you won't always be able to steer clear of all holes. Pick the line with the least holes and, once you have chosen your line, stick to it. Confidence is always key, so deciding mid-section that you are on the wrong line isn't going to help.

If you have a regular ride with some rocky sections included, then try different

Keep your wheels rolling to avoid the holes between rocks.

Keep head-up and focused on the exit.

lines every ride until you know which works best. This method of learning will mean that you automatically know how to adapt to a section that comes up on a trail you haven't ridden before.

Step 3: Rolling Wheels

As mentioned, riding too fast into a section of rocks is unlikely – rocks are one of the sections of trail where speed is your friend. You need forward momentum to carry your wheels over the holes and gaps between the rocks, so try to refrain from braking too much. By all means control your speed, but there really is a fine balance between being in control and making things harder than necessary.

Step 4: Don't be Intimidated

Rocks can be grippy; sometimes the most grippy surface you'll find on a trail. You should remember this when riding rocky sections, as it will remind you not to be intimidated by the sometimes fierce-looking rocks staring at you.

Step 5: Be Supple

Big rock sections may be daunting, but the worst thing you can do is to freeze up – to ride stiff – as this will only slow you down and make it more difficult to skim over the holes and gaps between the rocks. Your bike only has a certain amount of suspension, so don't rely on it to do all the work for you; suspension will

take the edge off the hits but you must still move your body weight with the undulating rocks.

It is best to let the bike move freely under you through rocky sections; as long as you are carrying some speed, not braking and are on a good line, you can let your wheels skip about a certain amount.

Step 6: Keep Your Head Up

As you are carrying your speed through the section of rocks, it is important to keep looking ahead and not at the trail in front of your wheels. Look down the trail and constantly make assessments about line choice. As you improve, you will learn to make decisions quickly about the

PROBLEM SOLVING

Some rocky sections on old trails or wet Welsh routes can include very slippery, shiny rocks. These are normally covered in moss and certainly not very forgiving if you fall. Look out for dense tree cover that will create constant shade; these areas will hide the most slippery of rocks.

There is no perfect way to ride a severely slippery section of rocks, it mainly comes down to confidence and commitment. You must judge whether you can ride with confidence and then commit to the whole section. Braking is only going to make things more difficult, so plan your line and be sure that there are bail-out lines if needed.

Remember that not *everything* is rideable; if you can't make it through, then don't worry, save your energy for the next technical section.

approaching rocks and the general condition of the trail, so don't push yourself beyond your limits now.

Training. As you will take a pounding from most rock sections, you need to be strong and ready for the hits. Upper-body, core and arm strengthening exercises will help.

Products. Snake-bite punctures (an instant flat tyre caused by the inner-tube being pinched between the tyre and the rim) most frequently occur due to sharp-edged rocks. One way to instantly lower your chances of a flat tyre is to increase the pressure in the tube; higher pressure makes it more difficult for the tyre to deform and therefore squash the tube. However, tyre choice is a better way to eliminate snake-bites. When you are choosing

your tyres, be sure to look for something with a strong casing; the side-walls of the tyre should hold themselves in shape. Lighter tyres (with thin side-walls) are tempting but they are not worth the hassle of the countless punctures that you can avoid with a strong tyre.

Further Skill: Jumps

Jumps come in all shapes and sizes. Some people love to jump and some love to keep their wheels on the ground. Jumping is great for fun, but it can also be a very useful skill to have – you'll be able to skip short, rough sections, for example. You must also work to have at least a basic grasp of jumping, for when you start to build speed on trails, small jumps will

Choose the right jump – start small!

WHEEL DILEMMAS

Your wheels may take a pounding from a rocky mountain bike ride – at the end you may find new dents, scrapes and wobbles. These simply cannot be avoided – by the nature of the sport, something has to give and it isn't going to be the rocks under your tyres. Most dents shouldn't be of any concern unless they are exposing the inner-tube, so don't worry about the aesthetics of your bike. Heavy hits on rocks may also cause broken spokes, again you shouldn't worry too much about one or two missing – you'll get home no problems – but try to replace them at the first opportunity and have a professional bike shop true (straighten) and re-tension your wheel.

occur naturally and you need to be able to control your bike if you leave the ground.

Step 1: Choose the Right Jump

If you want to learn how to jump, you should make things as easy and as safe as possible for yourself. Most trail-centres in Britain have practise areas with small 'table-top' jumps (a jump with a take off and landing that are bridged by a platform of dirt) – these are the safest jumps to practise on. Make sure there is a clear landing area, so that if you do get it wrong, you'll be able to bounce back and try again.

Step 2: Get the Feeling

It is best to get a feel for the jump before trying to get airborne. Approach the jump at a steady speed – just enough to make it on to the flat top – and roll up and over. Try this several times, so that you remember the feeling of riding up the take-off, across the 'gap' and down the landing.

There is no pressure to jump all the way to the landing, first try. Keep this in mind when rolling the jump and you'll be able to increase your speed only slightly

from your rolling pace when you begin to attempt the jump.

Step 3: Front First

As a continuation of rolling over the jump, you can now start to lift your front wheel as you leave the take-off. You don't need

Getting a feeling for the jump.

Practise with only the front wheel leaving the ground first.

to be going fast; if you've got enough speed to carry you up and over the jump whilst rolling, then you have enough to jump it.

As you ride up the take-off, let your front wheel follow the projection of the jump. The shape of the take-off itself should be enough to make your wheel leave the ground. Keep your arms strong;

Getting airborne.

on the handlebars, this is a common misconception about jumping; instead, you should use the shape of the take-off to naturally 'throw' you into the air.

Step 5: Body

Keep your body stable and central on the bike – your movements will be greatly exaggerated as you get momentarily weightless. Ideally you want your wheels to be level in the air. The shape that your bike makes in the air is dictated mainly by your position over the frame; lean back more on the take-off if you feel you are nose-diving and let your body weight move forward as you look to the landing, to stop your front wheel from lifting too much. These are only very subtle changes in position, so take your time and experiment gradually.

Step 6: Clear the Table

Now that you are confident with your wheels off the ground – this will probably take quite some time to achieve – you are ready to make the leap to jumping into the landing. The most important factor, as always, is to remain calm and confident. On a small table-top jump, there is not a huge amount that can go wrong, unless you get over-excited and completely clear the jump, which is not advisable.

Approach with the same amount of speed that saw your front wheel making it as far as the landing (before you started to get fully airborne). You should now be familiar with the technique of using the shape of the jump to launch you and your bike into the air. As you leave the take-off, spot the landing. Your body will generally follow your head, so looking at your landing spot should naturally direct you to it.

When you are mid-jump, your wheels should be level and you should be looking at the landing. The best landings are when both wheels mimic the shape of the down-slope (you may find this difficult to achieve at first, so don't worry about landing slightly rear-heavy to start with).

any jerky movements will just soak the jump up and make it more difficult to part with the ground.

As you come up and over the brow of the jump you should spot the landing. As you repeat the action of your front wheel leaving the ground, try to land the wheel into the down-slope. This will be smooth and the same action you are looking for when you are jumping.

Step 4: Parting Company

Once you have practised making the shape of the jump with your front wheel off the ground, it is time to part company with the ground altogether. The first thing to remember is that the flat table in-between the take-off and landing is there so that you don't have to jump all the way across first try. Begin by approaching with just a little more speed than before; now that you remember the shape and landing, this shouldn't cause a problem.

As you approach the take-off, remain confident and focused; remember that nothing can go wrong and that you have prepared well. You don't need to pull up

CHAPTER 6

TRAIL TECHNIQUES

Introduction

These are three skills that you can practise anywhere, any time and that will improve your overall riding ability by a huge amount. It is important to remember that one's skills can always be improved upon, so no matter how good you get at these skills, always continue to practise them and your overall riding ability will be aided.

Bunny Hop

To 'bunny-hop' is the term used for the technique that enables a rider to lift both wheels off the ground simultaneously. It is possible to use SPD pedals to get yourself off the ground (as being clipped-in to them allows an upward tug on the pedals to lift the bike). However, you should be able to hop the bike much higher with a good technique that isn't dependent on being clipped to the bike. This will enable you to clear objects and features found on any trail, and to manoeuvre and manipulate the bike to any position.

Step 1: Front Wheel Lift

The entire motion of a bunny-hop sees the front wheel lift into the air before the rear wheel, which then comes up to level with the front; so the front wheel lift is the first to be mastered. You are not looking to 'yank' the handlebars to lift the wheel; in fact this will have the opposite

Crafty skills can be practised anywhere and will help you along the trail.

effect and pull you towards the handlebars.

Pull on the handlebars but focus on a fluid 'roll' of your bodyweight backwards slightly as you do, with heels dipped for good body position. This will bring the front wheel off the ground with ease. Make sure to practise this until you are proficient and confident.

Step 2: Rear Wheel Lift

The rear wheel lifts off the ground using a 'scooping' motion on the pedals. To learn this technique, first try to lift the rear wheel alone off the ground. Stand up with your pedals level, heels dipped and rolling at walking pace. Make one fluid motion to move your bodyweight forward and point

ABOVE: *Front wheel lift.*

TOP TIP

Put your seat as low as it can go so that it is completely out of the way; otherwise it may inhibit your free movement for a good technique. Also remember that this is not a quick to learn technique, but once the motion 'clicks' in your mind, it will become easy and instinctive. Don't be disheartened if you don't get it straight away and never give up.

LEFT: *'Coiling up' before the hop.*

your toes at the ground, whilst pushing back on the pedals and lifting legs slightly. This takes some practise.

Step 3: Combine

Now it is time to combine the two. Roll your weight slightly rear, lift the front wheel and then thrust your weight forward, scooping the pedals as you do, so that the wheels lift to horizontal. Initially you are only aiming to get off the ground – don't expect to be hopping metres into the air. If you can lift the wheels one centimetre, then with further practise you will get higher.

Every time you are riding you should practise your bunny hops, they will serve as an incredibly useful technique whilst riding all trails.

Wheelie

The 'wheelie' is the technique to lift your front wheel off the ground whilst riding, and continue to move forward with the wheel in the air. Some people can wheelie for many metres but, whilst this is an impressive trick, it is not necessarily a useful skill. A short lift of the front wheel, though, can prove very useful, especially whilst climbing or riding flatter single-track trails to lift the wheel over objects on the ground, to move more weight to the rear wheel for traction and, when proficient in the skill, to aid with tight corners.

Step 1: Front Wheel Lift

Simply lifting the front wheel off the ground whilst riding is relatively easy – a pull-up on the handlebars will lift the front of the bike. For a good technique, you should follow the same rules as for bunny-hops: pull on the handlebars but focus on a fluid 'roll' of your bodyweight backwards slightly as you do, heels dipped for good body position. This will bring the front wheel off the ground with ease. Make sure to practise this until you are proficient and confident.

ABOVE: Front and rear lift combined into a bunny-hop.

BELOW: Basic front wheel lift.

Three-quarter pedal position ready for the thrust.

TOP TIP

Wheelies are easiest whilst riding uphill, as you won't pick up any unwanted speed and because your weight is already tipped slightly rearward over the back wheel. Find a gradually sloping, wide track and practise wheelies sitting down with your seat up at climbing height.

Advanced Brake Control

All quality mountain bikes are now equipped with hydraulic disc brakes, which are both efficient and extremely powerful. To advance your riding and overall flow on the trails, it is helpful to really get a feel for the power and also modulation of your brakes. Knowing how to slow down in a controlled and planned manner will allow you to only ever lose your forward momentum in planned amounts.

Step 2: Pedal Thrust

Rolling at very low speed and in an easy gear, position your cranks in the three-quarter position with the foot you would normally have forward (when coasting), at the top. Sitting down with the saddle at climbing height, push as hard as you can down on the pedal. You should feel the weight lift from your front wheel and you will be pushed backward slightly. Keep practising this until you begin to feel the front wheel really lift into the air.

Step 3: Pedalling

Now you have to combine the two.

Sitting on the seat and rolling at a low speed, pre-load your arms and then pull up using the front wheel lift technique. At the same moment you should push down hard with a power stroke. If the front wheel is coming up very quickly, then stop pedalling and, if you are about to lose balance completely, pull the rear brake to bring the wheel back down in an instant.

Once you master the timing of this combination, you need to think about

moving forward. This is simply a case of continuing your pedalling from the power thrust into a circular pedalling motion. Instead of focusing on your initial power stroke, which should begin to become instinctive, forward-plan to the following motion of your trailing foot. Again, if you are tipping over backwards stop pedalling and pull the rear brake.

Step 1: One-Finger Braking

With powerful hydraulic brakes you should be able to stop from any speed with only one finger on the brake lever, leaving the rest of your hand to grip the handlebars. Most people assume that the brake lever should be butted up against

Pedalling into a wheelie.

in a very short distance with just the front brake. To stop yourself from being lurched forward when you pull the brake really hard, retain strong arms and keep your weight to the rear of the bike to stop it from lifting.

Step 4: Quick Stop

Now combine your techniques with both brakes. Practise coming to a halt as quickly and safely as possible. Try not to get carried away, and always practise braking skills in a safe environment: soft ground, wide open space.

TOP TIP

You can get a feel for the power of your brakes without even moving. Stand with one foot on the ground and one on the pedal with the front brake fully applied. Your bike won't go anywhere. Modern brakes are very powerful and also very efficient. They are there to be trusted, not feared. That power will stop you in an instant – perfect for the moments when you round a corner only to find an unexpected surprise in the trail.

ABOVE: Using only the rear brake to stop

BELOW: This is an 'endo' – performed using only the front brake and a shift in body weight.

the grip, but this can make one-finger braking tricky, as the lever may come into contact with the gripping fingers. Move the brake levers into a position that leaves your remaining fingers free from interference.

Now practise controlling your speed with both front and rear brakes applied simultaneously, as you roll to a stop from a steady, but not excessive, speed.

Step 2: Rear Brake Control

To learn exactly how powerful your rear brake is, practise using it on a flat surface; preferably grass or soft ground with plenty of space. Roll at walking pace or slower, brace your body in a standing position and then apply only the rear brake. Keep doing this and trying to stop in a shorter and shorter space. The rear wheel may lose traction, so let go if you feel out of control.

Step 3: Front Brake Control

Practising with the front brake takes a little more delicacy, as you don't want to be thrown over the handlebars. Again, in a wide open area with soft ground under-tyre, roll at walking pace whilst standing up with pedals level. Do not jab the brake on. Instead, using only the front brake, come to a gradual stop.

Repeat at the same low speed but this time aim to stop in a slightly shorter distance. Continue to repeat this process until eventually you are confident to stop

PART 3
REPAIRS AND MAINTENANCE

CHAPTER 7

ESSENTIAL MAINTENANCE

Introduction

Keeping your bike well-maintained is vital to the machine's longevity and working regularly on your bike will aid your trust in it. As a beginner, the complex and intricate nature of the mountain bike can seem daunting, but in actual fact there are many checks and ways of maintaining your bike that are both simple and quick.

Quick Checks

It is sensible to give your bike a quick once-over before each and every ride. This routine will become instinctive after

RIGHT: Keep an eye on all moving parts.

BELOW: Check your bike over regularly for damage.

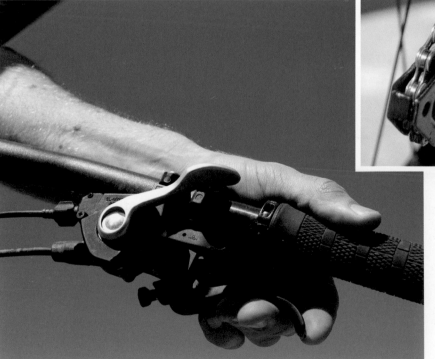

some time but to start with you need to remember several areas to check for wear and damage:

- *Chain:* if it looks brown and rusty, oil it; if one or more of the links are 'stuck', then you need to change the chain before further damage is caused.
- *Tyres:* a quick squeeze of each tyre prevents you heading out on a ride with a slow-puncture already in place.

- *Wheels and discs:* pick the front of the bike up and spin the wheel. Now do the same with the rear. They should both spin freely and without any friction or noise from the discs.
- *Suspension:* a quick bounce on the suspension, both front and rear, will soon tell you if anything is wrong. It's amazing what you can miss at the end of a long ride, so even if you think all was fine on your last ride, it makes sense to check.
- *Test ride:* have a quick spin on the bike and listen out for any creaks, squeaks or crunches. Go up and down through the range of gears to check they are indexing correctly.

Once you've gone through this process, which should only take a minute at most, you're ready to head out on the trails safe in the knowledge that your bike is in good working order.

A clean bike works better than a dirty bike.

Cleaning Your Bike

Mountain bikes are subject to huge amounts of mud and water – a clear occupational hazard for these machines – and they are built to cope with the punishment. However, the seals on bearings and all moving parts can only withstand mud and water up to a certain point, and the last thing needed is to age your bike further still in the cleaning process. Cleaning your bike sounds like a simple task, but follow these guidelines and your bike will last a lot longer:

- *Be swift:* however cold or hungry you are after a ride, try to forget about it for another 5 minutes; the sooner you start to clean your bike, the easier it will be, as the dirt and water will still be loose.
- *Apply water:* with a hose-pipe on a low-pressure setting, spray the entire bike to ensure that all mud/dirt is wet. This will make the rest of the job much easier.
- *Cleaning agent:* good-quality bike cleaning sprays are worth using as they really do help to dislodge dirt from every nook and cranny on the bike. Beware though, these all contain strong chemicals, so don't leave them on for more than a couple of minutes or they could dull your paintwork. Try to avoid using washing-up liquid, as it can contaminate your brake pads and will also break down any grease.

Oil your chain every time you wash the bike.

- *Loosen dirt:* use a brush to loosen the dirt and to create a foam if you have applied a bike cleaner.
- *Spray:* spray the bike clean and repeat the process if necessary. Make sure that there is no mud or debris in the gears, the underside of the saddle or in the steerer-tube.

- *Buff and lube:* use a dry, clean cloth to buff the bike and to prevent any watermarks being left. Run the chain through the cloth to dry any water and then use some quality lube, being sure to stay away from the rear disc when applying it. Lean the bike up against a wall and spin the pedals

backwards whilst applying the lube to the chain at the rear derailleur.

A clean bike is a happy bike and you will enjoy riding out of the door on each ride with a functional bike that has had some care taken to keep it in good condition. This job of cleaning your bike takes no more than 5 minutes, so it is worth doing as soon as you get home from a ride.

After-Ride Checks

Once you have cleaned and lubed your bike, you may want to think about performing several after-ride checks. These don't necessarily need to happen after each and every ride, but it is a good idea to include them in a weekly schedule to ensure the safety and long life of your bike:

Bolt check: check over every bolt on the bike – this won't take as long as it sounds – from handlebars to the rear derailleur. Bolts can easily be rattled loose on a ride, so make this a fairly frequent check.

Wheels: check your wheel quick-releases or bolts after every ride to ensure that everything is straight and tight.

Spoke tension: you can make a quick assessment of the spoke tension in the wheels simply by 'pinging' each spoke; listen to the change in pitch and check the spokes a pair at a time to feel for tension.

Air pressures: air suspension does lose a certain amount of pressure, so check the PSI of both front and rear units every five rides.

Creaks: with weight on the handlebars and feet on the pedals, bounce on the bike a little and listen out for any creaks. Creaks can be caused by dry bolt-threads, so once you have located a creak, take the bolts out (i.e. the four bolts that clamp the handlebars in place) and clean the threads. Replace and tighten the bolts and, if the creak still happens, seek further advice – it could signal a hidden hairline crack or problematic bearings.

ABOVE: *Bolt check.*

BELOW: *Check your tyres for signs of wear or any tears.*

Check the alignment of the derailleur and the cable tension.

Further to the above, a bi-monthly full strip-down of the bike is worth investing in. Take the bike to your local shop for this and expect to pay around £75. In a full strip-down the shop will remove any hidden mud from inside the bottom bracket and hubs, clean and grease bearings and threads throughout, tighten everything to exact torque settings and clean the drive-train completely. Your bike should ride like new and will last much longer.

Gears: Quick Tune

Cable stretch along with the constant rattling and general punishment that a mountain bike takes on each ride will cause your gears to go out of sync

every so often. This is absolutely fine and a one-minute tune up will usually solve the problem.

Step 1: Alignment

If the rear derailleur or the hanger (that attaches it to the frame) are bent or twisted, then you will need a bike shop to either straighten them with a specific tool or replace. Looking from the rear at the gears, check whether the hanger and derailleur are straight.

Step 2: High and Low

The high-low adjusters on the derailleur set the point at which the outermost

gears sit. Therefore, when in the top or bottom gear, the chain and sprocket should line up directly with the derailleur.

To set the rear gears:

*   Put in the smallest sprocket and then look from behind down the line of the derailleur. The jockey wheels of the derailleur should line up exactly with the sprocket.
*   If they don't, turn the cross-head screwdriver bolt marked 'high' and you will see the derailleur move into place.
*   The same applies for the low gears and for the front mech, which you should aim to be running with no rub from the chain as you turn the pedals.

ABOVE: *Sometimes the drive-train simply needs a good clean.*

BELOW: *Check your quick-releases are done up before re-aligning the brakes.*

Step 3: Cable

Assuming the high and low gears are set and everything is straight, the most common factor in affecting the working of your gears is from the cable.

Several checks should determine the problem:

- Is it rusty? If the cable is rusty, or muddy, then it won't be able to move freely through the outer-housing. Try spraying a little oil through the housing. If it still won't move freely, you probably need a new cable.
- If the cable is kinked in any place, then it also won't be able to move freely, which will affect the gears as you click from 1st to 8/9th. If there is a kink in the cable, you'll need a new one.
- Tension on the cable should be checked in the smallest sprocket; this is when the cable is not being loaded

by the shifter. Drop the bike into the smallest sprocket and then press on the exposed piece of inner cable near the derailleur. This should not be slack. If it is, undo the bolt that holds it in place on the derailleur and pull a little more cable through, until it is set taught.

- Barrel adjusters: these are used to fine-tune the gears. They are the small, black plastic dials that are on either end of the cable: one on the gear shifter and one on the derailleur. Twisting these anti-clockwise will put more tension on the cable in small increases, which makes it therefore easier to achieve a smoothly running drive-train.

Brakes – Quick Re-Align

Occasionally your disc-brakes will go out of alignment, which can cause a number of issues, such as noisiness/squealing and a shortened lifespan for the brake pads. This is not normally a big problem and is likely to happen simply due to the huge forces that the brake caliper and its fittings have to cope with.

To re-align a brake:

- First, loosen the two bolts that hold the caliper in place (which attach to the frame/forks). The caliper should be loose but not completely unattached.
- Pull the brake lever so that the pads clamp the disc.
- Keeping the brake lever pulled in, 'rattle' the caliper to ensure it is sitting on the disc.

Checking over the frame's welds.

- Re-tighten the two bolts and then let go of the brake lever.

Now the disc should be central within the brake pads; the clamping action whilst the caliper was loose centralizes everything. Spin the wheel to check that there is no rubbing and, if there is, then repeat the process. If there is still noisiness/rubbing then check that the disc is not bent.

Frame Safety Check

Checking the integrity of the bike's frame is not something you should have to do regularly, but it is worth having a quick look over the frame every five or so rides. You should also be looking for cracks in the rims (the wheels) and anything out of the ordinary. Creaks in the handlebars are certainly to be treated with extreme caution and any noisiness should be addressed immediately.

Look carefully over the joins in the tubes – the welds – for any hairline cracks. You really want to catch frame faults before a full frame failure, which could result in injury. Mountain bikes can only stand up to a certain amount of punishment, so frames do fail; fortunately, most major manufacturers will provide warranty services.

CHAPTER 8

BASIC REPAIRS

Introduction

Mountain bikes are complicated machines with a multitude of mechanical and hydraulic components, all of which need maintenance and occasional repair. Bikes must be robust without making them overly heavy, which results in components that can only withstand a certain amount of punishment; some breakages are to be expected.

Your bike will break at some point when you are out riding; however well-prepared or careful you are, it cannot be entirely avoided. Knowing how to assess and deal with the damage could get you to the end of a ride. This chapter explains some quick fixes for common problems that you will encounter when riding.

Bike fixes are mostly very simple.

Truing a wheel.

Basic Wheel True

When a wheel is 'true' it is completely straight and round; free from side-to-side wobble or up/down movement when the wheel is turned. Although you should technically be aiming to always ride with true wheels, once they have been used it is rather unrealistic for them to be perfectly straight again.

The simplest rule with wheels is to have an expert build them for you in the first place – there are dedicated wheel builders in cycling – as they will pay a huge amount of attention to detail regarding spoke and nipple length and tension, all of which will play a huge part in making wheels that will last years and not need a huge amount of attention. Even if you have bought your wheels pre-built, you should have a wheel builder re-tension them before and after your first ride; they will last a lot longer.

However, you may need to re-true your wheels once in a while, or for particularly heavy riding styles this may become more frequent. One rule to remember is that if the spokes are becoming loose after every ride, then your wheel needs a proper re-build and tension, so take it to an expert.

This home wheel truing exercise will not achieve perfect results, so don't expect absolutely true wheels.

Step 1: Set-Up

Without the use of a professional wheel truing stand, your best option is to leave the wheel in the frame/forks. You will need a marker to work from to gauge the buckle of the wheel so fix something in place; a zip-tie attached to the frame/ forks and cut to length will work well.

Using a zip-tie as a reference point to work from.

Step 2: Find the Buckle

With the bike upside down or in a work-stand, spin the wheel and look down its line to assess how straight it is. You are aiming to bring the rim back to a central point, so also consider where the centre on the frame/fork arch is.

Step 3: The Theory

The spokes are tensioned by twists of the nipples; the further clockwise that you wind the nipple, the more tension on the spoke. There are a certain number of spokes on the left and the same number on the right, so if both are tensioned identically, then the wheel should, in theory, be straight. By locating the buckle in the rim, you now want to use the spoke tension to pull the rim straight again.

Step 4: Bring it in Line

At the buckled spot, find the central spoke that is nearest to the buckle. Loosen this spoke by a quarter-turn and then tighten the two spokes either side

---

TOP TIP

You must not over-tension the spokes, as this can cause damage to the nipples, the threads of the spokes and ultimately the rim and hub. If you are turning more than two full turns on each nipple to straighten the wheel, then you should stop and seek expert advice.

---

of it on the opposite side of the rim by a quarter-turn each. Spin the wheel again and you should notice that the wheel has been pulled away from the buckle slightly. If there is still a noticeable buckle, then repeat or try working on a larger section of spokes; try loosening two on the buckle side and tightening four on the opposite side.

Cable Change

The cables that connect your gear shifters (on the handlebars) to the front and rear derailleurs are susceptible to problems caused by dirt and water that can get into the black outer cable. This dirt and water can cause the cables to get stuck and to

rust; both cases will make gear changes difficult.

There is not a great deal you can do to avoid this happening, so it is necessary to replace the cables every once in a while. When your gears are reluctant to down-shift, and certainly if you are finding it hard to push the shifter up through gears, then it is time to change your cables.

This is a simple procedure that you can do at home with only a set of Allen-keys and some cable cutters.

WHEEL WORDS

Spoke: the straight, round pieces of metal that support the wheel.
Nipple: the spokes screw into nipples that sit in the rim.
Hub: the central point of the wheel that sits on an axle through the frame/forks and that houses bearings, as well as attaching the spokes.
Rim: the outside of the wheel, a metal U-shape that the tyre and inner-tube sit into.
Rim tape: tape is needed to stop the inner-tube from being punctured when you inflate it – otherwise it would protrude into the holes that house the spoke nipples.

New cables only cost a few pounds from your local bike shop.

Spokes break regularly when riding off-road.

TOP TIP

Some gear shifters have differing ways of attaching the cable. On some SRAM systems you may have to take the shifter off the handlebars and open it up to fit the new cable. This is a simple procedure that is reasonably self-explanatory, but if in doubt, ask your local bike shop – they'll be happy to explain and once you've been shown once it will seem obvious.

Step 1: Remove the Old Cable

Drop the bike into the smallest sprockets at both the front and the back. Now detach the cable at the derailleur, which is attached via a 5mm Allen-key bolt. At the gear shifter end, you should see an exit hole for the cable (this may be plugged by a simple plastic screw so take this out if necessary); push the cable through the shifter and it will come out of the exit. If the cable is particularly rusted or kinked, then this may take a little force.

Step 2: New Cable

The new cable threads in exactly as the old cable came out. If you can't get the cable through the shifter, then you've probably changed the gear accidentally – the shifter must be in the bottom-most gear. If you are really struggling to get the cable through the black outer cable, then spray some oil in to try and shift any dirt. If you are still struggling, then check the black outer cable for any kinks – if there are any, then it'll need to be replaced as well.

Step 3: Tension and Cut

Once the cable is all the way through to the derailleur, give it a good tug to ensure there is no slack anywhere. Wind the barrel-adjuster fully in and then back out three clicks. (This will be helpful for later tuning.)

Now you want to tighten the cable to the derailleur; make sure you do this in the same way as it was attached to begin with. Holding the cable with pliers may make this easier but you don't need to pull lots of tension on the cable, it should be taut but not pulling the derailleur up the gears. Cut any excess cable and fit a crimp to ensure the cable doesn't splay.

Step 4: Adjust

Using the barrel-adjuster to tension the cable, adjust until your gears change easily and smoothly. After one ride you may need to re-tension the cable as it will stretch.

Broken Spoke

With all the ground hazards present on any mountain bike ride, your bike will occasionally take some punishment that cannot be avoided. Broken spokes are one of the problems that can arise and are one of the slightly trickier fixes, but can still be fixed at home with only a spoke-key and a spare spoke of the correct length (you will have to consult a local shop, as there are many different lengths). Spokes are very cheap, so it is worth having several spare in your toolbox – they normally cost less than one pound each.

TOP TIP

If you have tightened the nipple firmly and there is still no tension in the spoke, then you have either a wrong length spoke or nipple. It is for this reason that you can't just fit any old spoke to replace a broken one.

Step 1: Preparation

First, you will need to take the wheel off the bike; remove the tyre, disc and cassette, if on the rear wheel. Now that you have the wheel stripped down, you should be able to see how the broken spoke threads out at the hub – the head of the spoke will be either facing inward or outward, so take note. At the rim end of the broken spoke, lift the rim tape and you will be able to push the remaining piece of the spoke and nipple out at the hole.

Step 2: New Spoke

The new spoke needs to thread through the hole in the hub just as the old one came out. Cross the new spoke over and under other spokes in the wheel on its way to reach the hole in the rim (look at the pattern on the remaining spokes and copy). This may mean you need to flex/bend the spoke a little but don't worry. Push the new spoke through the hole in the rim and then thread a new nipple on with a little light oil on the threads.

Step 3: Tension

You will now need to re-fit the rim-tape, tyre and cassette, and then put the wheel back in the bike. With the spoke-key, bring the new spoke up to a similar tension as the rest of the spokes (judge this by squeezing two spokes together). Now you will need to stress the wheel by pulling each pair of spokes toward each other with a strong grip, this settles any imbalances. Finally, true the wheel.

CHAPTER 9

TRAIL-SIDE REPAIRS

Introduction

Breakages out on the trail are inevitable, but if you can't repair them, then how to get home? The simple answer is that you must be able to fix the problem or at least make the bike rideable to get you off the mountain and to safety. With nearly all breakages this is easily done, albeit with a little quick-thinking and ingenuity.

In this chapter you will find a selection of common trail-side repairs, but with some experience you will develop quick-fixes of your own – remember that you aren't aiming to get the bike back to perfect working order but simply to a rideable state so you can get home.

Broken Chain

The chain on a bike is under a huge amount of stress on every ride. Pedalling forces are hard on the chain, but also a lack of general maintenance and regular checks can lead to your chain breaking. Take care and inspect your chain on regular occasions for bends, stiff links or rust, and it will be far less likely to break whilst on a ride.

If your chain does break, it isn't a huge problem – don't panic. There are several easy steps to repairing a broken chain: you will need a chain tool (which should be included on any quality multi-tool) and a spare quick-link/power-link (which can be purchased for less than five pounds in any bike shop).

Re-fitting the rear wheel. Don't be afraid to push the derailleur out of the way.

TOP LEFT: *A broken chain link.*

TOP RIGHT: *Removing the broken link with a multi-tool.*

Step 1: Remove Broken Link

With a chain tool, place the chain in one of the grooves on the tool; this secures it in place. Wind the lever until the pin from the tool lines up with the pin of the chain; the simple job of this tool is to push one of the pins out.

MIDDLE RIGHT: *The chain; prepared for a quick-link.*

Step 2: Chain Prepared for Quick-link

Push the pin right out (this can be stiff but don't force anything – check you have the pin and tool lined up correctly), so that you end up with two 'ends' – holes – to the chain. Now the chain is ready to have a quick-link fitted.

Step 3: Re-Fit Chain

Thread the chain back through the front derailleur, around the cassette and then through the rear derailleur, so that both 'ends' to the chain meet up at the bottom of the bike. From here you can create extra slack in the chain by pushing the rear derailleur forward.

Push the rear derailleur forward to create slack.

'Clicking' the quick-link into place.

Torn Tyre

Tyres on modern bikes are very durable; however, they can still tear in some circumstances. If you don't repair the tyre before fitting a new inner-tube, then the tube will burst out of the tyre resulting in more punctures.

To fix a torn tyre, simply take the tyre off the rim and locate the hole. Use a piece of duct-tape to seal the hole, and layer it up if needs be. If the hole is more sizeable, use a piece of the old inner-tube to bridge the gap and then secure it in place with the tape.

This is not a permanent fix, but will get you home.

Punctures

The simplest and most frequent fix on a bike ride is the puncture. Everyone thinks that they know how to fix a puncture properly, but in fact most don't. With good technique you can avoid any further issues; heavy handed approaches can often tear or puncture the new or repaired inner-tube. Removing and re-mounting the tyre is the most important part of the process, so learn this well.

Step 4: Fit Quick-Link

Now push the two parts of the quick-link through the 'ends' of the chain, click the two pins through the widest hole and, with your thumb and forefinger pushing the chain link together, pull in opposite directions until the pins locate in the small hole. Make sure the link in the chain is free-moving before riding.

Step 1: Removing the Tyre

There are several ways of making the removal of the tyre much easier:

* *Let all air out of the tube:* even with a flat tyre there may still be some air left in the tube.

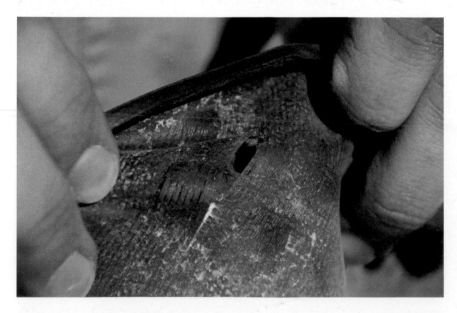

A torn tyre can usually be fixed.

RIGHT: Tape over the hole.

BELOW: Centre the tyre for easy removal.

- *Centre the tyre:* go around the entire tyre 'pinching' it with your fingers so that the beading is in the centre of the wheel rim – this creates the most slack possible.
- *Start near the valve:* the tyre will come off most easily near to the valve, so peel the tyre back and fit one tyre lever here, then use the second tyre lever to ease the tyre away from the rim.

Step 2: Assess

Now you must find the hole in the tube. Contrary to popular belief, you do not need a bowl or sink full of water to do this. Simply pump the tube up and follow around its entire circumference with the tube pressed close to your lips – you'll feel the air leaking at the hole. 'Quick-patch' kits are the best and easiest way to fix a puncture, as they eliminate the need for any glue – fit one over the hole.

Step 3: Check the Tyre

Turn the tyre inside-out and check around

Always check the tyre for thorns or tears.

its entire circumference. You are looking for any objects, such as thorns, nails or similar, that may have punctured the tube. Remove anything that is stuck in the tyre and then re-fit to the rim.

Step 4: Fitting the Tyre

Pump a little air into the new or fixed tube and fit it into the tyre (fit the valve through the hole in the rim last). Now go around the tyre pushing the tube into the centre of the rim with your finger-tips. This places the tube away from the rim, so that when re-fitting the tyre, you don't risk pinching the tube between tyre and rim.

Push the tyre back on to the rim, finishing near the valve to make the process as easy as possible. If you are struggling, go around the tyre and push

Push the inner-tube into the tyre to avoid snagging it when re-fitting the tyre.

> **TOP TIP**
>
> Tyre levers are sometimes necessary but can also play devil's advocate; use them wrongly to re-fit the tyre and they'll puncture your newly repaired tube. One way to lower the risk of re-puncturing is to only use plastic tyre levers – this will reduce the risk but not eliminate it. The only way to be sure, is simply to take your time and not to force anything back on.

the beading to the centre – just as you did when removing it – to create extra slack. Only use the tyre levers to re-fit the tyre if absolutely necessary.

Broken Seat

In the event of a big crash or, if you are particularly unfortunate, a heavy landing on the seat, often the seat can break off at the rails that connect it to the seat-post. This is not a major problem when you are near home or a bike shop, as new seats are reasonably cheap to buy. However, when you are out on a big ride, a broken seat can make the difference between riding home with ease or a potential emergency; riding long distance without being able to sit down will drain anyone of energy and could leave you stranded.

As with many trail-side repairs, solving the problem of a broken seat comes down to a little ingenuity and a certain amount of creativity. You don't have access to spares or a full toolkit, so use what you have in your bag instead. The easiest way to re-attach a broken seat is simply with an old inner-tube (one that you punctured earlier); cut the valve off if you have a knife and then, with the seat in place, wrap the inner-tube around the centre of the seat and downwards around the top-tube of the frame. Wrap the tube around until it is tight and the seat won't shift, and simply tie a knot around the length of the inner-tube.

Simple and not pretty, but this fix will save you a lot of energy on the ride home.

Bent Wheel

Only a handful of years ago, off-road wheels used to suffer with a lack of strength to their weight, which resulted in frequent taco-shaped wheels due to crashing or even something as simple as turning too hard in a corner.

Thankfully, modern wheels are sturdy, robust and lightweight, and don't bend or buckle anywhere near as much as wheels

Only use plastic tyre levers and try to avoid using them to re-fit the tyre.

used to. However, it does still happen, and with a big enough crash, your wheel can be turned into a Pringle shape. The fix for this problem is not pretty, but again it will get you home. Don't expect your wheel to ever be back to its original strength – once bent, the rim will need replacing – so only use this method to get you home.

Step 1: Remove the Wheel

Take the wheel out of the frame/fork and assess the damage; if the rim is badly cracked or split, then it may be time to call a rescue team, but it is still worth giving the wheel-fix a shot – you can't do any further damage after all.

Step 2: The Re-Shape

There is no pretty or correct way to do this – you are simply looking to manipulate the wheel back to somewhere near its original, round shape. You are unlikely to achieve perfect results; your goal is only to get the wheel round enough to spin in the frame or forks.

Using something such as a tree stump or a rock, create a lever to force against

by resting the hub on the object and one side of the wheel on the ground, with your foot to hold it in place. Now use nothing more than brute force against the lifted (bent) side of the wheel to attempt to force it back into shape.

Step 3: Assess

With each attempted re-shape, put the wheel back in the frame/forks to see how much further you need to push it. The more that you stress metal, the weaker it becomes, so try only to force the wheel into a shape that is enough to allow it to spin in the frame/forks and don't worry about getting it perfect – you won't.

Step 4: Tension

You can now attempt to use your wheel-truing technique to further pull the wheel back into shape; tighten the spokes on the opposite side to the bend and loosen the bent side, but only a quarter-turn at a time each. Amazingly the wheel can often regain its shape, but you must not be fooled – the wheel is greatly weakened and must be replaced before any further riding.

PART 4
FITNESS AND NUTRITION

CHAPTER 10

TRAIN TO IMPROVE

Introduction

Having a training routine does not have to mean going to the gym and exercising for hours on end in a room full of sweaty people! Mountain biking is a fun way to get fit or to increase fitness, but as you get more serious about the sport, you will want to train your body to cope with the stresses involved in everyday bike riding, and to help your body to relax and recover. This can involve home routines or exercises, some of which you will find out about in this chapter.

The Benefits of Training

Physical training and conditioning is beneficial not only to your health, but also to your ability on the bike. Being strong, flexible and energetic are outcomes of training and physical exercise – all of which will add to your handling capabilities. Your body is your engine, so it is important to treat it well. This also means that the bigger and more efficient the engine – the better trained your body – the faster and further you will be able to go.

Physical conditioning will help you on the downhills.

Types of Training Explained

Resistance

Resistance training involves working against a weight, force or gravity; it is often referred to as 'strength training'. Free-weights are one example of resistance training.

Increasing your strength will benefit the ease with which you manoeuvre your bike and will prolong the time that it takes fatigue to set in. Strength training can take the form of lifting free-weights and use of gym machinery but can also be put into effect using simple household items or body weight (press-ups etc.).

Interval

Interval training involves short bursts of hard exercise that work the aerobic and anaerobic systems; for example, five sprints punctuated by two-minute rests.

Interval training, or 'intervals', are very hard work and often forgotten from training routines, but they will increase your ability to react to situations, your ability to sprint and to be able to sustain a high level of energy output during a long period of work (i.e. a race).

Continuous

Continuous exercise is a longer period of relatively low-intensity work aimed at raising the heart rate and working the body's aerobic system. It is also referred to as cardiovascular or aerobic exercise. During prolonged exercise oxygen is constantly delivered to your muscles, thus 'aerobic'.

Endurance athletes train using continuous exercise to work their heart, lungs and, therefore, circulatory systems over a long period – this is normally fifteen minutes and above. The aim of continuous training is not to use your muscles' anaerobic capacity (the ability to turn glycogen into instant energy) but rather the aerobic system.

Being fit will make your everyday rides much easier and more enjoyable.

EXERCISE TERMS

Aerobic: the aerobic system converts carbohydrate and oxygen into energy for your muscles.

Anaerobic: anaerobic energy is obtained from stored glycogen in your muscles – the instant energy needed for sprinting or weight lifting.

Glycogen: glycogen is what your body converts carbohydrates into to be stored and used by your muscles. Glycogen is needed in all forms of exercise, particularly anaerobic.

Heart-Rate Monitors

Your heart is the vital organ that pumps blood around your body, the blood that carries oxygen and further fuel for your muscles to turn into energy. Keeping track of your heart's activity is a good way of observing your fitness and also the workload of exercise. Wearing a heart-rate monitor has several further benefits to aid in any training or exercise routine, and will help you to monitor your level of exercise, as well as your physical state before and after exercise.

If your heart rate is particularly high at resting (before exercise), then you may either be getting ill, still recovering from a previous training session (this may have been up to two days prior) or suffering from different outside influences – stress, nerves, and suchlike.

If you want to train seriously, or even just to improve the ease at which you ride your bike, then it is very helpful to know

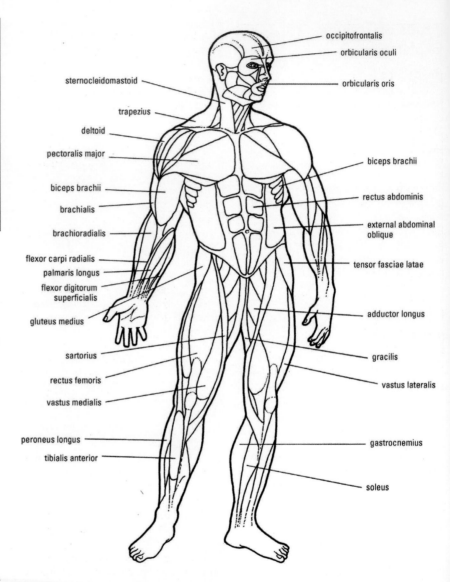

The most-used areas of a mountain biker's muscular anatomy.

DAY	HR AT START	TRAINING SESSION	MAX. HR REACHED	CALORIES BURNT
Monday	80	Cardio	160	400

Heart-rate monitors help to monitor your training.

your heart's beats per minute – cardiovascular or continuous exercise is performed at around 140–150bpm, and interval training aims to raise your heart rate to near maximum during a session, for example.

A Cyclist's Anatomy

Most people understand their anatomy and anatomical terms to a certain degree, but knowing which parts of your body are important when you are mountain biking will help you to train those areas.

Lower Body

Quadriceps. The large muscle at the front of the thigh. These are used in straightening the leg – the action that pushes the pedal down toward the ground.

Calf. The calf muscle is in the lower leg and works in opposition to the action of the quadriceps; it brings the foot back upward and the leg to a bent position.

Hamstring. The hamstring is in the back of the thigh and its action works with the calf muscle to pull the leg up, the foot back toward the buttock.

Gluteal. The gluteal muscle group is better known as the buttocks. The gluteus maximus and medius are used in the motion of pedalling to move your thigh forward, and are also necessary in keeping your body stable whilst sitting and moving the thighs.

Upper Body

It is a common misconception that cycling relies largely on the lower-body muscle groups; in fact the upper body is used extensively, particularly in mountain biking. Just think of all the pulling/lifting actions involved, especially when climbing, and add the stability needed to stand and descend, and you soon get a clear picture of the need to condition your upper body.

Biceps. The muscle at the front of the upper arm that performs a 'pulling' action. These are used to stabilize and to help you in the turning of the handlebars, as well as to lift or pull on the handlebars.

Abdominals. The abdominal muscles are around the core of your body – the 'stomach' area – and play the part of stabilizing and holding your body in position. These are worked extensively by mountain biking, especially on tough climbs.

Triceps. The triceps are located at the back of the upper arm and their primary function is in the extension of the arm. In mountain biking this aids stability and is necessary in reacting to undulating ground. Most mountain bikers have well-developed triceps – more so than the biceps – as they play the biggest part in holding you in a standing position on the bike.

Pectoral. The pectoral muscles are in your chest and, although less used than the biceps and triceps, play a part in holding the body stable whilst riding standing up. Downhill riders certainly develop bigger pectoral muscles due to increased time standing and reacting to undulating ground and heavy landings.

Forearm. The forearm plays a large and vital part in mountain biking. Containing many intrinsic muscles, as well as nerves and tendons, the lower arm (forearm) performs functions that twist and turn the hand, flex the fingers, support the wrist and support your upper body.

The Importance of Warm-Up Routines

One common misconception of the pre-exercise warm-up routine is that the term solely refers to stretching. On the contrary, stretches should never be performed from cold, and should only come after a warm-up or following exercise.

A warm-up is essentially a light session of exercise that should last at least fifteen minutes and should be performed before any exercise – this includes riding your bike. The aim of the warm-up is to prevent injury and, in doing so, to aid flexibility.

When you are going bike riding this could just mean riding at a slow pace for the first fifteen minutes and then stopping for a brief stretching routine (stretches before exercise are seen by some to be helpful in injury prevention but their primary function is in longer flexibility routines that take place after the ride or at home).

If you are training at home or in the gym, then take fifteen minutes at the start of your routine to go through some simple warm-up exercises, which can consist of almost any low-intensity and low-impact activity, e.g. jogging on the spot; skipping; rowing; exercise bike.

Basic Training Routine

Your training routine can take place on the bike or at the gym, and can consist of a variety of exercises. Your goal is to work different muscle groups and to balance your training so that not one area or side of your body is trained excessively. Remember that if you train your pectoral muscles, for example, then you should also work on the muscles in your back to create balance, just as you should work on both the biceps and triceps, not one or the other.

The key to training is to keep it fun and changeable – you don't have to do intervals every time you train if you are a downhill rider. Likewise cross-country riders should work on strength not just continuous exercise. Try to use the gym's weight machinery – the leg press being one example – as little as possible, as these machines isolate muscle groups to be trained specifically; using free-weights or exercises such as press-ups, squats and lunges use your entire body and develop the core strength and balance needed for real sport.

Flexibility

Being flexible and regularly stretching your muscles is an important part of any sport,

not least mountain biking; you'll have fewer injuries, less build up of lactic acid and you will feel less discomfort after hard rides. Stretching can also be very relaxing for the body and mind, so view it as a treat, not a chore.

Safe Stretching

Stretching can bring its own problems and potential dangers, so several guidelines must be followed; Only stretch after a warm-up routine or following exercise, and never push a stretch too far – you should only stretch to the point of feeling a slight pulling in the muscle and never jolt or force a stretch as this can lead to torn muscles and further damage. Stretches must be gentle, relaxing and certainly not uncomfortable.

Why Stretch?

The primary and most frequent use of stretching is in recovery exercises, and in this sense stretching will relax and elongate your muscles after a workout

BENEFITS OF STRETCHING

- Improve your circulation.
- Improve your flexibility and range of motion for targeted joints.
- Address muscle imbalances.
- Relieve aches and pains.
- Give you time to relax and 'switch off'.

(this can mean anything from a thirty-minute ride to a four-hour epic). This helps to deal with the strain and resulting wear on muscles and the inflammation that ensues.

From a training point of view, stretching and flexibility exercises help to avoid muscle imbalances, to improve balance and to develop good core strength. Stretching can, and should always, be incorporated into a training routine.

Lower-Body Stretches
Stretch 1: Calf

Stand facing a wall, feet shoulder-width

Calf stretch.

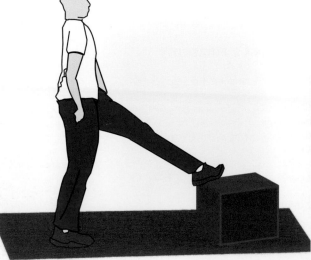

Hamstring stretch.

apart. Now reach out to place your hands on the wall at shoulder height. Take one leg backwards and place that foot flat on the floor with feet, legs and torso still facing forward.

Keeping the 'back leg' straight and foot flat on the floor, lean on to and over your 'front leg', so that you feel a slight pulling in the calf muscle of your 'back leg'. Switch to the other leg and repeat.

Stretch 2: Hamstring

Stand with one foot on a raised surface, leg straight – this can be anything up to hip height but, if your hamstrings are particularly tight, then do not try to push hard. If in discomfort, reduce the height.

Bend the other leg and you will feel a pull in the raised leg's hamstring. Hold, then switch legs and repeat.

Stretch 3: Hip Flexor

Kneeling, bring one leg forward so that you are in a lunging position and tilt your pelvis up as if to bring it towards your head.

Now move forward into the lunge – you should feel the stretch in your thigh and the front of your hip. Switch legs and repeat.

Stretch 4: Quadriceps

Standing on one foot, bring the raised foot backward and move the foot toward the buttock. Hold the ankle with one hand and pull the foot upward and into the buttock until you feel the stretch at the front of your thigh.

Hold, switch feet and repeat.

Stretch 5: Gluteal

Sit on the floor with legs outstretched, back straight. Bring one foot up level with the opposing knee. Now bring that foot over to the other side of the straight leg's knee.

ABOVE: Hip-flexor stretch.

TOP RIGHT: Quadriceps stretch.

Use your hands to pull the bent leg's knee up towards your body. You should feel the stretch in your buttocks. Switch legs and repeat.

Upper-Body Stretches

Stretch 1: Pectoral

Stand adjacent to a wall, hands by your side and feet pointing forward. Now raise the arm next to the wall to bring a

Gluteal stretch.

90-degree bend at the elbow, your hand resting on the wall.

Twist away from the wall keeping your palm flat against it. You should feel the stretch across your chest. Swap sides and repeat.

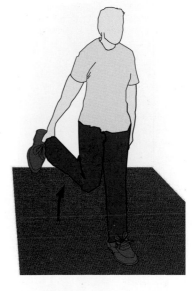

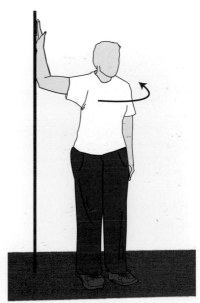

Pectoral stretch.

Shoulders stretch.

Lower-back stretch.

Stretch 2: Shoulders

(Note: The intention of this stretch is to connect your hands together behind your back, but not everyone is flexible enough, so it can help to have a towel at the ready.)

Standing in a relaxed stance, feet pointing forward, raise one arm up above your head and then bend at the elbow to reach down your back. At the same time,

bring the other hand up your back and try to link hands. If you can't reach, hold the towel between your hands to bridge the gap, but get your hands as close together as possible.

You will feel the stretch in your shoulders and upper-arms. Swap arms and repeat.

Stretch 3: Lower Back

Lie flat on your back, arms outstretched. Bring both knees up to a 90-degree bend with your feet still flat on the floor.

Now lay your knees over, both in the same direction, towards the ground. This must be a very gentle stretch. Lay your knees over to stretch the other side gently and then come back and push your knees further toward the ground. Repeat.

Stretch 4: Upper Back

Standing straight and relaxed, bring both hands up to chest height, arms outstretched straight in front of you. Clasp your hands together so that your fingers are interlocked.

Now, keeping hands locked together, push away from your chest and you will feel the stretch in your shoulder blades. Relax and then repeat.

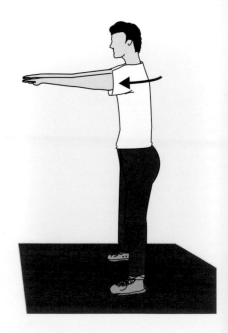

Upper-back stretch.

TOP TIP

Hold stretches for at least twenty seconds – anything less and the muscle won't have time to relax and react to the stretch. You can hold them for longer if you like; up to sixty seconds will be beneficial.

CHAPTER 11

HOME ROUTINE

Introduction

Training can be very beneficial to your performance in any sport, and gyms are a great place for specific training. But gyms are not to everybody's tastes; many people like the idea of the fitness boost but not whilst training in a public environment.

Training at home can be fun and more easily accessible. Setting yourself a routine from home gives you the choice to tailor your gym to your own preferences and particularly to incorporate features that you may not find at a public facility.

In this chapter you will find several fun and effective exercises that will not only boost your fitness but also your ability on your bike. Make these exercises a regular part of your weekly routine and you will soon see your riding improve.

Using Household Items

Try to think of ways that you can use items in your house in the place of regular gym equipment; most of which is only designed to imitate everyday actions anyway. One example is to use old drinks' bottles as weights; fill them with water and you have a good light weight for multiple repetitions. You can change the filling to increase the weight, if you like (fill with sand, pebbles or anything dense). These free (of charge) weights utilize items that you may otherwise throw away and can be used for lifting exercises or for jogging on the spot to increase the workload.

Turbo-Trainers/Static Bikes

Spinning classes have become one of the most popular activities in gym timetables,

and for good reason. Sitting on a static training bike for any period of time can easily be tailored to give you a harder workout than cycling outdoors for the same period of time, as you will have no rest periods on an indoor bike – no downhills, flat sections or tail-winds for rest.

However, without the wind rushing through your hair, you may also get a sense of working far harder than you in fact are – you'll notice a lot more sweat without the wind to dry you.

A 'turbo-trainer' is a cycling reference to a piece of equipment that you sit any ordinary bicycle into – it clamps around the rear wheel and provides resistance against the wheel via a metal roller. These are best used with a slick or low-profile tyre to reduce the amount of noise

produced. For around £100 you can acquire a good turbo-trainer that will see you through a winter training regime and even if only used for half-an-hour daily, you will notice your fitness improve.

Turbo-Trainer Use

You can use your turbo-trainer in many different training routines and the advantage, when compared to riding outdoors, is that you can tailor the 'ride' down to every minute, second and heart beat. It is a lot easier to keep a constant heart-rate on the turbo-trainer, as there are far fewer variables, and you can focus on retaining a heart-rate as opposed to avoiding cars, trees and rocks. You can

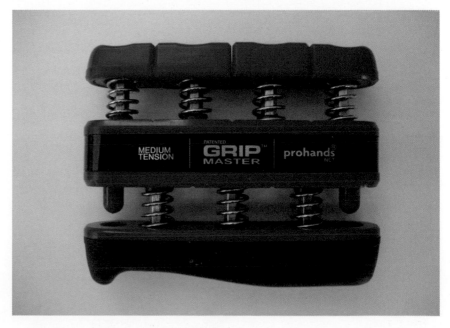

A hand and forearm strengthener.

use the turbo-trainer for sprint, stamina building, fat-burning, low-intensity and any session you wish.

Arm Pump

A slightly strange sounding term albeit, but 'arm-pump', technically known as carpal tunnel syndrome, is a major problem for many mountain bikers. This term refers to the loss of feeling/strength in the lower arms and hands, which usually occurs on longer downhill sections and can be increased by factors such as cold weather and fatigue. Arm-pump is a result of the tendons and ligaments swelling in the carpal tunnel – a sheath in the wrist that houses all the ligaments and tendons – resulting in a pressure build up and ensuing loss of strength and feeling.

There are many ways to combat arm-pump. In the most extreme cases, some athletes choose to completely alleviate the possibility through surgery that increases the size of the carpal tunnel. But don't fear – there are far simpler and less extreme measures to take first and

> **TOP TIP**
>
> There are other types of static devices that can be used, some more advanced cyclists prefer 'rollers' – a system that supports both wheels, the rear wheel spinning the rear rollers that are attached via a band to the front rollers that therefore spin the front wheel as you pedal. This system gives a real sensation of riding the bike and it is down to your balancing skills to stay upright; not an easy system to master.

that solve the problem for the majority of riders.

Arm-Pump Exercise 1: Hand Clamp

Specific hand-strengthening devices can be found in any climbing shops and can be bought in grades so that hand strength and stamina can be increased at a steady rate. These clever devices can fit into your pocket and therefore can be used

anywhere, at any time. Work on individual fingers and your whole clamping action and work on the amount of repetitions that you are able to perform. Making notes on your performance is important so that you can monitor your progress.

Arm-Pump Exercise 2: Home Set-Up

A common exercise used not only by the keenest of mountain bikers, but also by the majority of Motocross racers (who really do battle with arm-pump); it can be done at home using some everyday objects from around the house.

You will need:

- A plastic bottle.
- String.
- A stick or old pair of handlebars.

First, fill the bottle with water, then tie one end of the string around the bottle and the other end to the middle of the stick/handlebars. The simple aim is to 'reel' the bottle up to hand level and back down again using an alternate twisting action with your hands. This sounds easy but your arms will soon tire and begin to seize.

With regular training – which you can do with any spare five minutes – your hands and arms should soon strengthen and condition to the stresses of long descents. This problem can never be entirely alleviated, so don't be deterred if you continue to suffer on long downhills – just remember that everyone else has the same problem, so the best you can do is to train your arms as much as possible.

Balance Boards

Balance boards are simple and fun. They are essentially a skateboard deck (i.e. with no wheels) suspended by a round or tubular object. The idea is to stand on the board without over-balancing in any direction; a good exercise for your balance, coordination and core-strength, all of which will increase your bike-riding abilities.

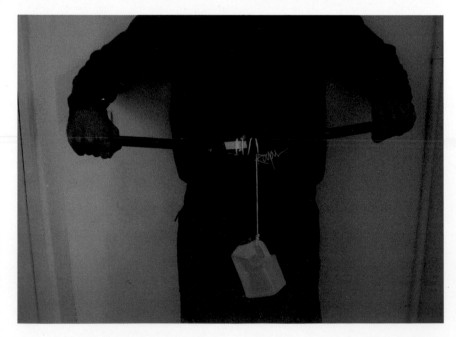

Arm-pump exercise number 2.

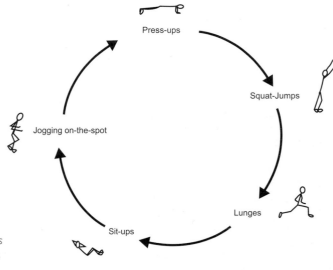

TOP LEFT: Cool Board make the best balance boards, but they are expensive.

TOP RIGHT: Home circuits example routine (for each of these exercises you should perform as many repetitions as possible within a minute). Repeat this process for a monitored length of time (i.e. the same length of time for each session) and you will be able to take note of how you are improving as your fitness increases..

Balance boards can be used at all times – for instance, whilst relaxing in front of the TV. Five, ten or fifteen minutes will be beneficial and many people find themselves relaxing through use of the board – in a similar way that yoga helps one to relax and unwind. In addition to standing on the board, it can also be used for a great number of exercises – place your hands on the board whilst doing press-ups for example and your core stability will be pushed more than a standard press-up.

Make Your Own Balance Board

The best balance boards can be bought from good sports shops or online and use basketballs or small plastic balls to balance on (these are called 'Cool Boards'), providing a challenging task to stop the board tipping in any direction. However, these can be expensive, so one option is to make your own from an old skateboard.

You will need:

* An old skateboard deck.
* A large plastic bottle.

Fill the plastic bottle with water and you have your base – the board pivots atop the base.

How to Use Your Balance Board

* Place the board on top of the plastic bottle (in a safe environment – carpeted floor and no tables/chairs/doors, etc. in the near vicinity). Start with one end of the board resting on the floor; this is the ground-foot.
* Now rest the other foot lightly on the other end of the board; this is the top-foot. Apply a little pressure to the top-foot and you will feel the ground-foot lift slightly, the board will try to slip out. Take the pressure off the top-foot and you will stop moving.
* Get a feel for the manner of the board and then, when feeling confident, push down with the top foot so that the board levels out and both ends are suspended. The idea is to now stay off the ground by counteracting any potential over-balances.

Many top athletes use balance apparatus to improve their balance, core strength, focus and simply to relax.

Home Circuits

'Circuit training' refers to a set of exercises laid-out in a loop, or circuit, which are repeated non-stop for up to an hour. It is normal to have up to ten different exercise stations in a circuit training layout, each of which comprise anything from sprinting on the spot, to lifting weights, to press-ups.

Circuit training is both popular and physically demanding. Its popularity is down to the great all-round workout that a session provides and the fact that the participant is not 'slogging away' at one exercise for a prolonged period; normally you will stay on each exercise station for no more than one minute.

Most gyms provide a daily circuit training session run by a coach, and working out with a group can drive some people to try harder. However, there is no need to go any further than your living room for circuit training. Set up your own routine incorporating several of your favourite and not-so-liked exercises and your fitness will profit.

CHAPTER 12

NUTRITION

Introduction

Nutrition in sport is as important as having the correct equipment; without eating and drinking sufficiently and healthily, your judgement, focus and performance will falter. When riding mountain bikes the last thing that you need is to be lagging in energy levels – you need every bit of concentration that you have.

This chapter outlines the benefits of a good diet, as well as explaining a good dietary plan and how to prepare not only for hugely exerting rides, but also your everyday ride. Pay particular attention to hydration; a drop in food supplies can be counteracted by your body's fat supplies for quite some time but if you don't hydrate efficiently, you will soon suffer the effects.

Benefits of a Good Diet

Eating well and keeping the amount of alcohol you consume down to minimum will not only serve as a great benefit to your health, but also to your sporting performance. Your body is your engine when biking, so putting the wrong fuel, or food, into your engine will hinder its performance and slow you down. A good diet should include a balanced mix of carbohydrates for energy, proteins for body repair and plenty of nutrients. You should also be consuming a lot of fluids; at least 1.2ltr a day and more if you are exercising or it is hot (as we lose fluids through evaporation when we breathe, sweat and pass urine).

Food for Fuel

Your body needs food – food is the fuel to power all bodily functions, especially during sporting activity. Much poor information is transmitted through fad-dieting plan ideas that suggest cutting out vital parts of a rounded diet; some even tell us that we should stop eating carbohydrates. On the contrary, our meals should be well-balanced, with fuel from all food groups.

Hydration

Your body is made up of up to 60 per cent water; this should act as some sort of advisory for how important water is to us. Typically, cyclists say that if you feel thirsty, then it is too late – you are already dehydrated. It is absolutely vital to start a ride well-hydrated, to hydrate whilst riding and to continue to take on fluids during recovery. The easiest way to tell if you are well hydrated is by the colour of your urine: pale yellow and clear means you are hydrated; dark yellow means you are dehydrating – but you'll probably already be feeling other effects anyway (headaches, cramps, fatigue and light-headedness.)

Drinks

If you are riding/exercising for less than one hour, then the best drink is water; it will provide all the hydrating benefits you need. You do not need specific sports or carbohydrate drinks for exercise periods shorter than this. For rides and training over one hour in length, you will benefit from specific sports drinks, as they provide carbohydrates and electrolytes (which help the body to absorb water efficiently).

Drinks available on the supermarket shelf and labelled 'energy drinks' – fizzy and sugary caffeine drinks – do contain some useful ingredients, but in huge quantities. The best option is to consult your local bike shop for information on the best drink for the distances you are covering, as they will be able to provide powders that have been scientifically developed with performance in mind for before, during and after your ride.

Pre-Ride Nutrition

Good foods to eat before riding include carbohydrates (wholegrain bread, porridge, pasta, etc.) as these stock your energy supplies. Before endurance events, athletes like to 'carbo-load' – which means to stock the body's glycogen (energy) stores as much as possible – to ensure sufficient energy stored for a sustained effort. Carbo-loading does not mean that you have to eat twice your average calories before an event or ride; instead, you should simply increase the proportion of carbohydrates in your diet for three days before the ride.

During-Ride Nutrition

During a ride of any length you should be drinking plenty of fluids, but you also need to keep your body fuelled with sufficient carbohydrate. The body can only store enough glycogen to sustain itself for 90min of exercise without additional

---

PRE-RIDE FOOD IDEAS

Cereal or porridge with milk; wholegrain breads and pastas; peanut butter; brown rice; rice cakes; dried fruit.

carbohydrate intake, which means that you must feed at regular intervals on anything longer.

You need to take in lots of carbohydrates, but not in big chunks, as your body will struggle to digest a large amount of food and will subsequently slow down any other processes; eat little and often. You also only want to take foods that you know you can eat and enjoy – there is absolutely no point taking an energy gel that you hate the taste of because you will only avoid eating it and therefore risk a drop in energy or an eventual 'bonk' (when you completely run out of energy, also called 'hitting the wall').

As far as hydration goes, you need to drink water and other fluids for any exercise session longer than 40min – wait any longer and you will quickly dehydrate, in which case a drop in performance will be the least of your worries.

After-Ride Nutrition

It is easy to assume that when the ride stops, the need to nourish stops too. This is in fact absolutely wrong and feeding your body the correct fuel directly after a ride is the most important part of good mountain-biking nutrition.

As soon as you finish a bike ride, your goal should be good recovery. This means replenishing and repairing your energy stores and damaged muscles. The first thing to remember is not to reach for a 'refreshing' beer – alcohol opens up the blood vessels leading to increased inflammation of the muscles and therefore a longer recovery period, as well as interfering with your body's attempts to

replenish energy stores and, furthermore, dehydrating you.

Protein is often thought of as the most important aspect of recovery food and it is vital to our body in re-building and repairing any damages, as well as aiding in the uptake of water to rehydrate the body. However, more vital is the intake of carbohydrates to replenish your body's glycogen stores. As soon as you finish a ride, your body goes into overdrive in an attempt to rapidly restore its vital stores of energy – glycogen – ready for the next ride/bout of exercise. It does this in the first 30 to 60min following exercise, so it really is of utmost importance to take in as much carbohydrate as possible as soon as you stop.

Most nutritionists agree that a ration of 4:1 for carbohydrate against proteins is correct. The mix of protein with your carbohydrate is also thought to aid the body in the storage of glycogen.

Remember that hydration comes before all else – your body cannot function when it is deprived of fluids, so you should be taking in plenty of water for the rest of the day following your ride. Specific recovery drinks are worth the cost, as they will provide all of the carbohydrates, protein and electrolytes that you need without unneeded fat and calories.

Nutrition in Racing

When you are racing, it is very easy to forget or avoid eating; it can feel like

you are wasting time in doing so. However, if there is any time that it is important to be taking care of your nutritional intake, it is during an event. You must stick to the important rules of pre, during and after ride nutrition detailed in this chapter and apply them to your event schedule.

It may seem difficult to take on foods whilst in the race, but you should learn to do so efficiently and quickly – practise eating on the bike if you must – so that you don't risk running out of energy three-quarters of the way into the race. If you take care of this and make sure to keep taking on carbohydrates and water then you will be in the privileged position of being able to watch many other competitors drop in speed or completely give up, sometimes only half way into an event – this happens at every race simply because other racers don't understand the importance of fuelling the body and mind.

PART 5

COMPETING

CHAPTER 13

OVERVIEW OF EVENTS

Introduction

People have been competing since the very first days of the mountain bike. A largely non-competitive fraternity, the modern-day mountain biker does not rely on racing for absolute enjoyment of their sport, but most do attend events.

Racing is meant to be fun, and in mountain biking that ethos is vital. Events often have a serious front, with a percentage of the competitors taking part with a view to obtaining a high place, but a large number of racers are also in it purely for the fun and social aspect.

There are events to suit all styles, levels and tastes, so study this chapter well and decide for yourself how you would like to approach competing.

Why Race?

Competing at any sport can bring additional drive and motivation to practise and train regularly; one of the major motivations to take part for most amateurs. Mountain bike events themselves, however, are seen by many competitors as a social occasion; a gathering of bike enthusiasts and the opportunity to ride on a new course alongside hundreds of like-minded folk.

There are as many, and in fact many more, different types of events as there are disciplines within the sport. There are downhill, cross-country and trials events, but then within those categories there is a multitude of varying formats for competition: endurance, Enduro, single-speed solo, 24h team … the list goes on.

Take care to study the differing titles for events and make sure that you are entering the correct race for your level

The spoils of victory.

Enduro racing uses the best mountain bike technologies on a downhill course.

and aspiration. Remember always that racing is fun – don't make it a chore for yourself and if it is, then take a break. Champions enjoy what they do and so should you.

Different Race Disciplines Explained

With so many differing events across all the disciplines, which one to go for? Below is a brief of the various styles of event that you may find on the calendar. Note though that, as mountain bikers love diversity and a new challenge, there are always new ideas coming about for events, some as far-fetched as 24h

downhilling on a floodlit mountainside, long-distance single-speeding and racing through the streets of Welsh towns.

Downhill

An entirely downhill course, which is set to test riders technically, as well as physically and mentally. Competitors race against the clock individually. Race times are usually between two and five minutes.

Cross-Country

A mass-start event with an unlimited number of competitors in each race start.

Courses are a loop, normally consisting of technical features and wide-track pedalling. Events are usually around twenty to thirty miles in length.

Enduro

The new-school discipline, this event combines downhill and cross-country racing in an attempt to divine the best all-round mountain biker. The formal format is that of a stage race; competitors must pedal up the hills to a start point in a limited amount of time to avoid penalties. Each stage is timed individually and is, for the majority, downhill. Events consist of up to eight stages over a weekend.

Single Speed

As with single-speed riding in itself, these events cater for those wishing to have the most fun, or to prove a point. Similar in format to a cross-country event, power and sprinting skills are needed to muscle up steep climbs. Often tracks are mostly single-track.

12/24 Hour

Twelve and twenty-four hour races take place over several days and often have a 'festival' atmosphere. The course is laid-out in a loop and the aim is to complete the most number of laps in the time limit.

- *Solo:* some riders like to put themselves to the test by entering as an individual, and seasoned professionals can ride for the entire event without stopping.
- *Teams:* consist of two to eight riders who take it in turns, relay style, to ride as many laps of the circuit as possible.

Endurance

Not to be confused with Enduro, these events are a test of sheer endurance in the form of an extended cross-country race, often around 100km.

Mega Avalanche

The name of one particular event in the French Alps has become synonymous with this format. Riders start en masse at the summit of a mountain, often on glacier snow, and race down the entire hill with the aim of arriving at the foot first. Events are usually won in around 1h, but slower competitors can take up to 3h.

Levels of Competition

In mountain biking there has long been a lack of real structure to the events calendar, but this is improving. Within the sport there are now clear divisions between levels of competition, which are detailed below.

Local. Small, local events are the best to enter as a first-time or amateur racer; they are friendly, cheap to enter and mostly non-serious. A good way to find your feet or for a fun weekend outing.

Regional. Regional events, such as the Mini Downhill Series or the Southern Cross-Country Series, are a stepping-stone to the national stage. Although mostly amateur, some serious competitors do turn up. Don't be deterred by this, though, as plenty of people will still be there solely for fun.

National. The British Downhill Series is a largely élite level series with many of the world's top racers taking part in each event; but it is still open to all levels, as long as you reach minimum criteria. National cross-country events are more low-key, still frequented by a number of top professional athletes, yet welcoming to all comers.

International. There are many European and world-wide events open to all comers, which are detailed on the UCI (*Union Cycliste Internationale*) calendar. Be sure to check the entering criteria and method; some events only allow a certain number of foreigners, some are only advance entry and so on.

World Cup. The most important collection of events on the calendar, the Annual World Cup Series takes place from March until late September at locations across the world. Some events showcase all disciplines, but often the downhill and cross-country races will be on different dates, in entirely different locations.

Ranking Points

BC Points. These are awarded to competitors at all BC (British Cycling) sanctioned races (nearly all regional and certainly all national events). BC points' rankings are used to determine which category you should be racing in and you will be promoted through the categories if you have gathered enough during the season.

UCI Points. These are only awarded at UCI (*Union Cycliste Internationale*) sanctioned races. These races must fit a certain criteria in order to be sanctioned by the UCI, and in Britain only the national series will qualify. (UCI events will always be clearly indicated in event listings.) UCI points are needed in order to obtain a world ranking that will allow a rider to compete on the world stage.

Where to Find Out About Events

All regional, national and international level events are advertised in most bike magazines, as well as being listed in event calendars, usually placed in the rear pages. All sanctioned events are also listed on an official internet database on the UCI and BC websites.

THE GOVERNING BODIES

BC
In order to compete at nearly all races in Britain, you must be registered with the BC (British Cycling). This membership covers your insurance for competing, as well as many more benefits, so is worthwhile as well as compulsory.
www.britishcycling.org.uk

UCI
The UCI is the *Union Cycliste Internationale*; the world-wide governing body for all cycling-based sports. The UCI headquarters is in Aigle, Switzerland and for that matter they operate in French, but it is a multi-national organization. All international events are sanctioned by the UCI and also some national events.

www.uci.ch

CHAPTER 14

STARTING OUT IN RACING

Introduction

If you think that you like the idea of racing on mountain bikes and you have entered an event, then it is time to start thinking about your approach. There are many facets of race preparation that will help you not only to ride at your best, but also to enjoy yourself as much as possible.

When starting out, you don't want to put yourself under unnecessary pressure, so be sure to go to any event with a view to enjoying yourself. Try to persuade your riding friends to enter with you and then make a weekend of it; travel together, camp out and enjoy the thrill of racing. With this formula, your riding will improve dramatically in no time and you won't even notice it happening.

Which Event for You?

With so many different titles for events, how should you know which one is for you? The simple answer is that there is no right race; most mountain bikers will compete in a range of disciplines from downhill to night-time endurance events. Be sure to enter an event of according difficulty (for example, do not start off by entering a national series downhill race), but try your hand at a range of events until you either specialize in one discipline or find that you would rather continue to enter varying event styles.

Pre-Race Preparation

Once you have entered several events it will become important to start a regular routine – it will help you to relax knowing that you have ticked everything off – but to begin with it will help to know how to prepare and what to take. Although different events require different approaches, the majority of the ritual is the same.

Proper preparation prevents poor performance.

This is a useful motto to remember, and having this in your mind at all times should drive you to arrive at an event ready to race and be reassured by the knowledge that you have covered all possibilities. From the moment you enter the race you should start thinking about every possible scenario that could occur and how to prepare accordingly.

Mid-Week Food

The amount of thought that you put towards food preparation before an event can vary dependant on the style of race, but there are some rules that apply to all disciplines:

- Carbo-loading: this term refers to 'loading up' your body's glycogen (energy) stores before an event and is most important for endurance-based events, but is sensible for any weekend of racing at all. (Read more in Chapter 12 Nutrition.)
- Fluid intake: it is vital that you do not arrive at an event already dehydrated, which is easily done if you are busy thinking about every other factor. Your hydration routine could start a week before the event; the sooner you have your body functioning at its best, the better.
- Morning food: on the morning of an event, you should have a healthy breakfast. This does not mean that you must eat as much as possible or anything out of the ordinary though. Your body loves routines, so try to feed it with something similar to your normal breakfast and aim for a similar time.

Start competing to start improving!

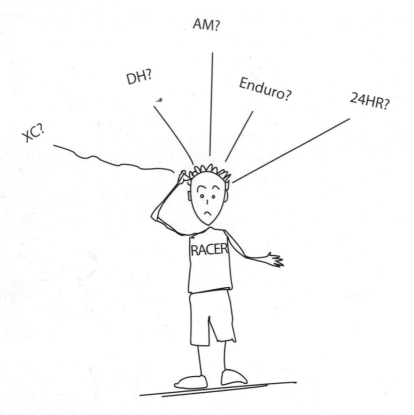

Choosing the right race can be confusing.

on your bike but don't worry if you don't own absolutely every tool as other people at the race will be happy to help you out.

Packing for the Event

When packing your bags for the event, make sure to be prepared for every possible circumstance. That means that you take waterproofs, even if the forecast says sun, you take spare gloves, lots of socks, several base layers and so on.

Navigation

Research how to get to the race at least the day before the event. With satellite imaging courtesy of Google, there are no excuses for not knowing how to get there. Arriving late and under added stress is not a good idea.

Sleep Well, Not Necessarily Lots

It is common sense to get an early night before an important event, but if you go to bed several hours earlier than you usually would, then the chances are that you won't be ready to sleep and will only therefore make yourself more nervous. Go to bed at a

Bike Check

You should be going to the race knowing that you have prepared for any mechanical faults on the bike. The last thing you want is to have a great effort ended abruptly due to a poorly functioning machine. So make sure you have cleaned, oiled and checked over every part of your bike. Don't leave this until the night before the event!

Spares

If you have a mechanical failure whilst practising at the event, you do not want it to cut your day short. So be sure to have a sensible amount of spares for the bike: inner tubes, a chain, gear cables and even a spare set of

tyres (most experienced racers take mud-specific spares as well). Also make sure you have the tools to work

Don't forget to check over your bike and to take small spares such as brake pads.

sensible hour and enjoy the prospect of riding your bike the following day – it'll be fun.

Morning of the Race

Wake early with plenty of time to relax and to have a casual breakfast. Eat oats and dried fruit for carbohydrate to fuel you through the day. Get into your riding kit when you feel like you are ready to ride – don't rush anything, just focus on the task ahead of you.

The Race Routine

When you are arriving at your first bike race you may feel like a stranger in a crowd of seasoned athletes who have far superior knowledge and experience than yourself. But don't fret; everyone has

TOP: *Taking a full toolkit and work-stand is not vital, but useful if you own it!*

BOTTOM: *Make the most of practise time but don't wear yourself out.*

been in your shoes as an amateur. Don't hesitate to ask questions, directions or for any sort of help; everyone will be glad to spare their time.

Both professionals and keen amateurs will have their own personal routines and approaches to an event, and as a new-comer to the racing scene it will give you a great step-up if you understand the simple processes that are involved in a race meeting.

Practice Routine

Arrive at the race with plenty of time to arrange your kit and food for the day. The first thing you will need to do is to sign-on at the registration tent, where you will need to present your racing license, if you have one. Look at the timetable for the event to find out when the practise sessions are. Practising well is as important as anything you have done in preparation for the race.

Use time in between practice and racing to relax.

Gravity Event Practice

All gravity events (i.e. downhill, enduro, etc.) have designated practise sessions in which to learn the course. For gravity events, learning the course is of paramount importance – your race is won and lost on seconds and fractions of a second, so you need to know every rock, corner and tree on the course. However, simply riding the course as many times as possible will not help. A good practise routine involves first walking the course – that is, walking from the start to finish and making mental notes – and then riding the course several times before walking it for a second time (with a better gauge on your speed of approach and which lines you are most likely to take). After this you can practise again, and by now you should be linking most of the course up in correct order in your head.

Cross-Country Event Practice

Fitness-based events (i.e. cross-country, endurance, 24h, etc.) require less knowledge of the track and certainly necessitate that you save all your energy for the race, but that is not to say that you needn't practise. You should only ride one lap though and don't get over-excited or you will regret it when your legs are failing in the event.

On your practise lap think about places on the course that require maximum effort – steep climbs, wide sections where you are open to be overtaken, etc. – and make a mental note to conserve energy before them. Also note where you will be able to overtake other people, so that when you are following and looking to pass, you can set yourself up for a clean, efficient manoeuvre. If there are any short, sharp climbs, then remember that a burst of energy and a gear change will be needed there. Finally, assess lines around any boggy sections, puddles, big rocks, etc., that are likely to slow you down, waste energy or potentially cause a mechanical failure to the bike.

Down Time

Any time in-between practise sessions and/or racing should be used for several things:

- Rest. Try to relax and sit down to save energy and give your body and mind some rest; your focus will benefit greatly.
- Bike check. Check over every single bolt on your bike to ensure nothing has worked loose – the last thing you want is for a pedal to fall off on the start line.
- Fuel. Eat some food – not too high in sugar and nothing like pastry or bread with refined flours, as they will slow you down mentally and physically. Energy bars are good, as are fruit and a small portion of pasta.
- Hydrate. Drink some water and a cup of tea to warm up and relax, if you like.
- Visualize. Think through the course and any racing tactics you think you may employ.

The Race

In the moments before the race, you should have one last check over your bike: check tyre pressure, clean any mud off and ensure nothing is loose. Next, you need to warm-up – a good warm-up lasts around 15min and will leave you not only warm, but also supple and focused.

Warm-up routine:

- Ride: ride your bike around the pits/near the start area for up to 10min to spin your legs and get your muscles familiar with the feeling of riding.
- Stretch: spend 5min articulating your joints and stretching muscles.
- Focus: your warm-up should be solitary and a chance to get 'in the zone' for the race; you can switch off from socializing and the pressure of the event and focus on the task in hand.

Following the warm-up you should be thinking about your race tactics and your lines/overtaking spots. You will be called to the start line normally around ten minutes before the race – although some cross-country races will call you forward before this time. Don't waste any time checking out the opposition – first appearances can be deceiving and those with all the new kit won't necessarily be fast. Therefore, don't worry about everyone else; this is your race and you can only do your best.

As you leave the start – this applies to all disciplines – focus on riding as well as you can, smooth but fast. In cross-country events, you should be thinking about where to use your energy and where you are going to be conserving it. In gravity events, you want to be hitting the lines that you practised – hit these smoothly, never panic and pedal hard on the easy sections in-between and you will ride faster than if you are thrashing at the handlebars and pedals.

Pace Yourself

Always pace yourself – riding at 100 per cent or above your limits never pays off. In downhill you will only make mistakes and in cross-country events you will waste all your energy, as well as risking mechanical problems. The key is to find a balance between speed and a smooth, flowing ride. Top downhill racers often comment that they in fact ride at only 80 or 90 per cent in races.

Only in the last moments of a race – this could be the final half-lap of a cross-country race or the moment that the finish line comes into sight in a downhill – can you really give it your all. This is the moment to dig deep, to use every last bit of energy and to make any overtaking manoeuvre you have been saving.

In downhill events, each rider will often have two timed runs down the course: one in the morning and one late in the afternoon. Use the time between runs to compare your race time against other peoples, and set yourself a realistic amount to improve in the second run. Think about any mistakes you made and also how tired you were. If you were exhausted straight away, then calm down and ride smoothly. Likewise, if you crossed the line still feeling fresh, then you didn't put enough effort in.

After the Race

Once you have crossed the finish line, you will have to wait for all the other riders to complete the race. Nearly all events have a live timing system that means you will be able to view the results as soon as everyone has finished. Note your result and try to get a print-out to take home for future comparison – this will help you to improve quickly.

If your routine comes together you will soon be moving through the ranks.

CHAPTER 15

IMPROVE THROUGH RACING

Introduction

Improving your race performances isn't only beneficial to your results but also a great way to gauge your overall improvement as a mountain biker. There are many ways to improve your racing – riding and practising more being the most obvious – but breaking each event down into small chunks that can be studied and diagnosed will also help greatly.

Making notes on your event performance, through analysing statistics such as heart rate, can help you to gain an understanding of your physical state and how you need to improve through training and physical conditioning, but gaining a simpler understanding of your ride on the day is harder. Through a series of note-taking and analytical performance breakdowns, this chapter will help you to understand your ability and how to improve quickly.

Analysing Your Race Performance

Knowing your weaknesses is one thing, but it is important to first understand which areas there are to improve upon. The following is a breakdown of the elements that make a good racer and therefore an efficient bike rider; you can use these to analyse your own performance:

Racing experience brings with it a quick improvement of skills.

- Technical skills.
- Composure.
- Fitness.
- Focus.
- Drive.
- Preparation.
- Tactics.
- On-the-day organization.
- Performance chart.
- Bike set-up with chart.

Technical Skills. Your ability on the bike. References to technical riding in a racing situation mean the harder, challenging sections of the track. Skills' practise and a lot of time on the bike will improve your technical ability. Think about how you rode the tricky sections – were you smooth or out of control? Were you going too fast and therefore crashed? Or perhaps you felt that you were so smooth you could have been going a little faster?

Composure. Your overall composure during the weekend of racing affects everything you do and, ultimately, your performance. Were you calm or feeling pressure and nerves all weekend? If you are worrying, then you won't be getting all the necessary tasks done or riding to your best ability.

Fitness. How was your fitness during the weekend? Even a pure downhill race requires a huge amount of fitness – not just for the race itself, but to also make it through an intense weekend of travel, practise, keeping your bike running and

socializing. The overall race experience is great fun but can be very taxing, so every bit of fitness helps.

Focus. How focused on the task in hand were you? This doesn't mean telling yourself to focus, it must come naturally. If you want to race well then you must go to the race weekend thinking only of the main event.

Drive. Did you feel a general, motivating drive all weekend? This applies to organizing your equipment, food and hydration. If you were lacking drive, then try to think why. Perhaps a poor night of sleep or a change in diet was the reason? Never blame your own motivation – if you are at the race in the first place, then you are keen enough. A drop in motivation on the day is always due to outside factors.

Preparation. Was there anything that you needed at the race that you didn't have? This could be something as simple as a sports drink or a fresh pair of socks. Note anything down for reference and make sure that it gets packed in the future.

Weekend Organization. Did you know your start time and did you arrive at the start line with plenty of time to spare? Small things can make a big difference to your performance, especially if they are making you flustered just before your start. If there was any way you could have improved, make a note for the future.

Tactics. How were your tactics during the race? Did you ride the lines you had practised, make passes in the best places and use your energy efficiently? Is there anything you can practise before your next event?

Bike Set-Up. How did your bike perform during the weekend? Did you notice yourself lagging on any particular sections due to excess rolling resistance from the tyres for example? You need absolute trust and confidence in your machinery, so note anything that may have hindered you and work on it before the next event. Bike set-up tips can be learned from anyone at the race, so don't be afraid to ask for tips on tyre pressure, suspension set-up for the course and so on.

Charts

It is a very good idea to keep track of your performances and the best way to do so is with charts in which you can score yourself for technical riding, fitness, motivation and so on. With these charts you can then monitor your improvement and gauge any factors that may have affected your ride on the day. Not many racers keep track of their performances but rest assured that the most successful most certainly do.

EVENT	PREPARATION	FOCUS	DRIVE	ENERGY	FITNESS	RESULT

This physical performance chart can be copied and filled in after every event to allow for comparison between performances and personal fitness. Note the event name in the left-hand column and then score yourself out of five for each of the titles (Preparation, Focus, etc.).

EVENT	CORNERS	TECHNICAL	JUMPS	RESULT

Fill in this table to analyse your technical ability on the day. If you made mistakes in some corners, score yourself lowly. By using this table you will be able to keep track of your progress and know what areas to work on.

How to Improve

There are of course non-specific ways in which to improve between races. Any time spent on the bike will boost your fitness and your ability, although there is a balance to be met, so if you are tired and finding it tough to motivate yourself to get out, then you should take a break. Riding with energy and enthusiasm once a week will see you improve far more quickly than if you try to force yourself out every day.

Timing

Timing yourself whilst riding a particular section or track is one way of gauging your improvement over long periods, but you will need to always time yourself in similar conditions or make note of the trail conditions that day and compare them against similar days.

There are several ways to time yourself, from a wrist-watch, which will give reasonably accurate times, to a professional timing device, such as a Freelap system. You can time yourself on your favourite loop as training for cross-country or on the hardest descent for downhill practise.

But there is no reason not to use opposing disciplines to help you to improve in one area; for example, racing yourself around a cross-country circuit is also going to benefit your downhill abilities, just as technical riding will improve on your cross-country racing skill-set.

Timing yourself a lot will give you motivation to improve, something to work against and is also vital racing scenario experience.

Training

Improving your fitness will improve the way that you are able to handle your bike and it will boost your concentration and focus.

If you are racing in cross-country or fitness-based events, then you may want to invest in a heart-rate monitor, which you should wear during all training sessions and races. This way you can gauge not only your fitness on the day, but also your recovery rate.

Try to combine fitness training with fun riding – sprints around a circuit are far more satisfying than in a gym, for instance. Again, with a heart-rate monitor you will be able to see how hard you have been working on any ride, thus combining your everyday fun ride with training.

Specific Skills Practise

Try to single-out any weaknesses in your day-to-day riding; which bits do you struggle the most with? If you can't get up a certain tricky hill climb, then keep trying it until you do or go on a ride one day with the sole intention of conquering that section. Likewise, if you always struggle with confidence on slippery tree roots, then make sure to practise, practise, practise until you are not phased by anything.

Certain skills will improve your race times no end; think about how many corners you have to take on every ride or race and then it should become fairly obvious that this skill is absolutely key. Good, flowing riding, especially through turns, will save you energy, time and will win you places. Also, work on your circular pedalling, pumping and line choice (try different lines through the same section and see how they affect your ride), as these will all help in every ride and race.

Cross-Training

You want to be a proficient mountain biker, but does that mean that you must put every ounce of motivation and effort into mountain biking only? Not at all. In fact, it is incredibly important to use other sports as training and respite – this is called 'cross-training' and there isn't a sports-person alive who doesn't employ the method. Cross-training ensures that you are always keen and motivated to be on the bike, it develops other vital skills (balance, stamina, etc.) and it is fun.

Try to use sports that are similar to mountain biking; any cycling-based sport will work to your benefit, skiing and snowboarding both use all the same basics (speed perception, weight transfer, balance).

Any sport at all will improve your fitness and therefore enjoyment of mountain biking, so join up with clubs or associations, enter that running race you've always wanted to do and don't be frightened to give the bike a rest!

Goal Setting

Goal and target setting is a vital part of progression for any athlete or sports-person. Setting yourself a long-term goal and then breaking that down into short-term, manageable targets, is one way to monitor progress and to motivate yourself to continuously improve.

Think about where you would like to be with your riding and racing in six months' time. There may only be one particular skill that you would like to master or perhaps you would like to improve by ten places in the events you are entering. You need to set yourself a definite goal to aim for and stick to it; you could write it down and stick it somewhere you will always see it to motivate you.

The next step is to break your goal down into the elements that will make it achievable; these will be your targets. If you are aiming to be better at sprinting to the finish-line, then you will clearly need to work on your sprints, but also

your fitness during the whole event – this will affect your last-minute dash for glory. If you have struggled with technical sections and aim to be able to ride them with ease, then you should spend less time training in the gym and instead put all your energy into attempting tricky sections – you'll still be riding a lot and therefore improving your fitness anyway. If your goal is less clear – you simply want to improve by ten places – then you need to set yourself a routine/regime that will see your gradual improvement.

Whatever your goal, you need to break it into targets – monthly or weekly – and focus on one target at a time.

Work on all areas of your riding and use race experience to aid your progress and you will soon be riding like this!

GLOSSARY

Allen-keys Tools to tighten most bolts on a mountain bike. Also occasionally called 'hex-wrench'.

Apex The mid-point of a turn.

Artificial Trail Most trail-centres have entirely man-made trails designed to cope with all weather conditions and to provide maximum fun.

Baggies Loose-fitting clothing (as opposed to Lycra).

Berm Banked turn.

Bike Bag A large bag used to transport bikes on flights.

Bike Rack Car fitting used to transport bikes externally.

Braking Bumps Ripples in the ground caused by the effects of braking. Can turn into bigger holes.

Brake-jack Difficulties caused by the effects of braking against the suspension's action.

Bottom Bracket The bearing that allows the cranks and pedals to turn in the frame.

Chain rings The front drive sprockets.

Cranks Connected to the pedals to allow drive.

Doubles Jumps with a take-off and landing but nothing in-between.

Double-Track Wide section of trail.

Dual-ply Tyres that have double-lined side-walls for extra strength.

Drift Wheels sliding.

Drop-off A vertical drop on the trail.

Flattie Flat tyre.

Flats Flat pedals with no clipping-in mechanism.

Flow A smooth, flowing ride with no stop-starts and fluid motion through the corners, etc..

Forks Front suspension.

Frame The main-frame of the bicycle. Connects all moving parts.

Grips Handlebar grips.

Mech Derailleur (gear changer).

Mineral Oil Mineral oil is used in many hydraulic brake systems, some use synthetic oil which is also found in the suspension units.

Multi-Tool Small foldable tool that includes most important tools for a mountain bike.

Trails/Trials The term 'trails' refers to the single-track paths ridden by mountain bikers, 'trials' is the technically challenging discipline that puts riders against a highly difficult course.

Uplift Transport to the summit of a hill/trail.

Rim The outer perimeter of the wheel.

Roots Tree roots.

Shock Suspension unit.

Turbo A turbo-trainer is a device used for static indoor training.

Quick-link Connecting link in the chain.

USEFUL INFORMATION AND CONTACTS

BC (British Cycling)
The governing body for all British cycling races and events. The BC provide rider and equipment insurance, instructor training, a database of events and publish a monthly newsletter to all members.

Web: www.britishcycling.org.uk

UCI (*Union Cycliste Internationale*)
The governing body for all international cycling events and affairs. Based in Aigle, Switzerland.

Web: www.uci.ch

Mountain Biking Wales
Website for information and helpful tips on all things mountain biking in Wales.

Web: www.mbwales.com

7 Stanes
The name for the main hub of Scottish trail-centres.

Web: www.7stanesmountainbiking.com

Places to Improve your Mountain Biking

Morzine, France
Every British mountain biker's home from home, Morzine is the most popular bike resort in Europe. Over twenty lifts open for bikes from June till September.

Web: www.morzine.com
Holidays: www.ridersrefuge.co.uk

Finale Ligure, Italy
Top destination for autumn and spring mountain biking. All types of cycling and mountain biking covered by the vast network of trails and mountain bike companies.

Web: www.comunefinaleligure.it
Holidays: www.finalefreeride.com

Granada, Spain
One of the best winter mountain bike destinations in the world. Rural villages and flowing single-tracks high up on mainland Spain's biggest peak..

Web: www.andalucia.com/cities/granada
Holidays: www.switch-backs.com

INDEX

RELATED TITLES FROM CROWOOD

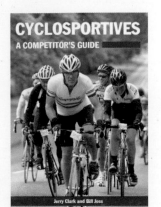

Cyclosportives
A Competitor's Guide

Jerry Clark and Bill Joss

ISBN 9781847972446

144pp,
160 illustrations

Starting Cycle Road Racing and Time Trials

Mark Barfield and Dr Auriel Forrester

ISBN 978 1 84797 014 5

128pp,
80 illustrations

Triathlon
Crowood Sports Guide

Steve Trew

ISBN 978 1 84797 170 8

96pp,
100 illustrations

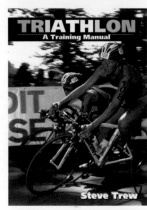

Triathlon
A Training Manual

Steve Trew

ISBN 978 1 86126 386 5

224pp,
80 illustrations

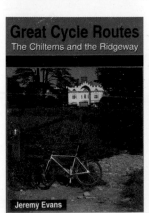

Great Cycle Routes
The Chilterns and Ridgeway

Jeremy Evans

ISBN 978 1 86126 029 1

96pp,
50 illustrations

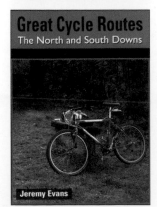

Great Cycle Routes
The North and South Downs

Jeremy Evans

ISBN 978 1 85223 850 6

128pp,
50 illustrations

In case of difficulty in ordering, contact the Sales Office:

The Crowood Press Ltd, Ramsbury, Wiltshire SN8 2HR UK

Tel: 44 (0) 1672 520320   enquiries@crowood.com   **www.crowood.com**